THE Active Life Cookbook

CONTENTS

Introduction   1

Up-and-Go Breakfasts   13

High-Energy Snacks   61

Healthy Lunches   109

Power Smoothies   157

Nutritious Dinners   205

Easy Entertaining   253

Index   302

INTRODUCTION

Unless you are living a purposefully slow life (think tree change, sea change) these days then chances are you are living an active one. Juggling work, family, friends and play is sure to put the pressure on the time that's available to prepare and cook food. That's one kind of active we address in this book. This book is also for people who step their active lives up to the next level, perhaps choosing to get involved in team sports at the weekend, an early morning kayak or run during the week, or a hike with the family on a Saturday morning. These fun activities are good for the body and soul, and often go hand-in-hand with a mindful attitude to food and what is being put into the body.

Fuelling the body adequately for an active life is not a complicated task. It comes down to eating plenty of protein, the essential building block for keeping bodies strong and healthy; choosing good fats with omega 3 fatty acids to protect the brain and heart (think olive oil, nuts and avocadoes); and, of course, a diet that's full of vegetables, especially the green ones.

It seems we know more about food these days than ever: 'superfood' is a household term; high-street supermarkets all boast health-food aisles that stock matcha tea and chia seeds and buckwheat flour; food intolerances are at an all-time high, and the gluten-free, sugar-free, dairy-free alternatives are everywhere. In this book, we provide recipes that reflect those contemporary trends, so you will find buckwheat pancakes and quinoa porridge in the breakfast section, but we don't neglect the everyday omelette or baked beans either. The principle of bringing together current trends with the foods and cooking methods that most of us know is reflected in the pages of this book.

Likewise, in the high-energy snacks section of this book you will find snacks for a quick sugar hit, such as peanut caramel chocolate bars, alongside raw buckwheat bars or nutty apricot granola bars, also delicious when your body has learned to appreciate them, that will offer a slower release of energy for busy bodies that need to keep on-the-go all day, every day.

If the words 'quinoa', 'raw' and 'buckwheat' make you want to head for the nearest fast-food joint, fear not — we have included plenty of information in the book that will help you navigate these foods and trends in simple terms and plain English.

Lunchtime recipes focus on salads — not the lettuce-and-tomato kind, but those with substance and amazing flavours. Salads with noodles, quinoa and cannellini beans will help power you through the afternoon and into evening. Polenta is an ingredient that features in this section as a nutritious alternative to potato. It's so versatile, going from creamy to crunchy depending on the method of preparation. It's a great food for eating on the run in its crunchy, sliceable form.

The section on smoothies provides fantastic options for a speedy and delicious hit of healthful nutrients to help you hop, skip and jump through to 5pm. Smoothies are deceptively simple to make, despite the complex-sounding menus of smoothie and juice options that feature at many cafes, and if you master the basic ingredients as outlined in the recipes here, you should be able to mix and match to make your own creations in no time.

Active

[ac·tive] **adjective**

characterised by action rather than
by contemplation or speculation
<an active life>

— MERRIAM-WEBSTER

As any mindful eater will know, the oft-quoted advice is to 'breakfast like a king, lunch like a prince and dine like a pauper'. With that in mind, we've presented some lighter options for dinnertime, such as soups, salads, stir-frys and fish or chicken dishes. But there are also some more substantial dishes that are high on protein, such as a pork tenderloin roast and even the occasional pasta dish (a carb-loading option for before an intense workout perhaps).

Even the healthiest, most active person needs to kick back and relax every now and again, and the recipes in the entertaining section of this book will help you do just that. We've kept it easy. We know you are busy and short on time, so the recipes you will find here present wonderful, fresh, healthy ingredients in recipes that are easily achievable. The feature foods in this section include mushrooms — so much energy in one little vegetable; raw fish — not just for restaurants, this is something you can prepare at home; and the antioxidant powerhouse that is the humble little blueberry.

In this book, you'll find a great mix of recipes from the classic to the contemporary, and we hope each recipe will present a helpful option for fuelling you through the day (or night). We've mostly kept it simple, but also offered a few more complex meals for when you have a little more time on your hands.

We hope you enjoy getting the most out of a cookbook that's been specially designed to reflect your active life.

Enjoy *The Active Life!*

Up-and-Go Breakfasts

LEMON IN THE MORNING

Perhaps you've noticed in the media advice to drink lemon juice and warm water first thing in the morning. It's not exactly hard to do it, but why bother? Seems there are a few good reasons.

HYDRATION

First, hydration. Okay this is just about the water, but it seems adding a squeeze of lemon and creating a ritual around it may be just the extra motivation needed to make drinking water in the morning a healthy habit. Make sure it's warm water as this helps flush the digestive system and rehydrate the body. If you are an active person who works out in the morning, drinking lemon water is a great way to rehydrate after a workout. It's just as effective as a sports drink, and with none of the nasties.

GETTING MOVING

And then there's poo. Water is a natural lubricant that softens things that need to be softened and the acid in lemon helps kick the digestive system into action, so water with lemon in the morning can help get things moving if help is needed.

MAKING YOUR DAY

Once the bodily functions are dealt with it, it's time to get on with the day. Lemon water may be able to help thanks in part to the vitamin C that it contains. Vitamin C boosts the immune system, helping keep infection at bay. It also assists the body in the production of collagen, which can prevent wrinkles, helping you to look and feel your best. Lemon juice contains an important mineral, potassium, which helps with brain function, ensuring you are bright as a button when you arrive at the office. Not only that, but it's thought that lemon may reduce the uric acid in our joints, a cause of inflammation, so that a cup of lemon water may reduce everyday aches and pains.

LOOKING AND FEELING GOOD

There may be no way to eradicate morning breath, but lemon can improve matters. It combats bacteria in the mouth, reducing its impact and freshening the breath. The weight-conscious will find a friend in lemon too. Some say the pectin it contains causes us to feel full and therefore eat less. Either way, drinking lemon water is a low-calorie option as compared to any other drink, except water itself. For the health-conscious, lemon has something to offer too. It is known that the liver can make more enzymes out of lemon juice than any other food, and this can help give your body greater energy.

Zucchini and Carrot Fritters

THESE HEALTHY AND VERSATILE FRITTERS ARE SIMPLY BURSTING WITH GOODNESS: A GREAT BREAKFAST OPTION

SERVES 2

300g (10oz) zucchini, grated and squeezed to remove moisture

200g (7oz) carrot, grated

100g (3½ oz) cabbage, finely chopped

2 eggs, beaten

½ cup (60g, 2oz) almond meal

2 tbsps flax seeds

1 tsp sesame seeds

1 tsp sea salt

1 clove garlic, minced

¼ cup (10g, ¼ oz) fresh parsley, finely chopped

¼ cup (60ml, 2fl oz) olive oil for cooking

2 tbsps sunflower seeds, to garnish

In a medium bowl, mix together all the ingredients, except the oil and sunflower seeds. Make sure all ingredients are thoroughly combined.

Heat half the oil in a large frying pan over a medium heat. For each fritter, spoon the mix into the pan and flatten with a spatula. Cook for 3 minutes until firm on one side, then flip over and cook on the other side. The fritters should be slightly crisp on the edges and golden in colour. Add more oil for cooking as needed.

Stack your cooked fritters on a plate and scatter over some of the sunflower seeds for garnish.

Tomato Omelette

WHAT BETTER WAY TO START YOUR DAY THAN WITH THIS
SIMPLE AND TASTY PROTEIN HIT?

SERVES 2

6 eggs

⅓ cup (80ml, 3fl oz) milk

125g (4oz) butter

½ red onion, chopped

3 Roma tomatoes, halved and sliced

1 cup (125g, 4oz) Cheddar cheese, grated

2 tbsps parsley, chopped

2 tbsps chives, chopped

In a large jug, whisk eggs and milk together. Season to taste.

Melt half the butter in a frying pan over a medium heat. Add red onion and fry for 4-5 minutes, until soft, then add the tomatoes and stir for a few minutes until soft. Transfer to a bowl and set aside.

Wipe out the pan with paper towel. Melt the remaining butter in the same pan over a medium heat.

Add half of the egg mixture. When almost set, spoon on half the tomato mixture and add the cheese. Fold over and cook for 1 minute. Slide onto a serving plate.

Repeat with the remaining ingredients for the second omelette.

Sprinkle the omelettes with parsley and chives, and serve.

Cauliflower and Spinach Fritters

A CLASSIC BRUNCH DISH WITH CAULIFLOWER ADDING CRUNCH AND A FRESH TWIST TO THE HUMBLE FRITTER

MAKES 8 FRITTERS

1 small head cauliflower, chopped into small pieces

2 cups (60g, 2oz) fresh spinach, chopped

2 spring onions, finely chopped

3 eggs, lightly beaten

½ cup (60g, 2oz) chickpea flour

2 tbsps flatleaf parsley, finely chopped

1 clove garlic, crushed

1 tsp salt

Freshly ground pepper

2 tbsps olive oil, for frying

¼ cup (50g, 2oz) Greek yoghurt

Boil the cauliflower in large pot for 4 minutes, until softened. Drain and mash it well but do not puree it.

In a large bowl, combine the spinach, spring onions, eggs, flour, parsley, garlic and salt. Give it a good couple of grinds of pepper as well. Add in the cauliflower and mix well. Shape small handfuls of the mixture into balls and flatten slightly.

Heat a dash of olive oil in a large frying pan on medium heat and fry the fritters a couple at a time. Don't overcrowd the pan. Cook on each side for 5 minutes or until browned all over.

Serve with a side of fresh Greek yoghurt.

Egg Cups with Ham & Tomato

SERVES 2

Oil or butter, for greasing

4 slices ham

2 Roma tomatoes, sliced

4 large eggs

Salt and freshly ground pepper, to taste

Preheat the oven to 200°C (400°F, Gas Mark 6).

Lightly grease 4 muffin trays with oil or butter. Press a slice of ham into each muffin cup (you want the ham to hang over the edges of cups). Crack an egg into each cup and arrange tomato slices over the top.

Transfer to the middle shelf of the oven to bake for 12-15 minutes until whites are cooked but yolks are still runny.

Season eggs with salt and pepper and carefully edge them out of the muffin trays.

Frittata with Cherry Tomatoes

SERVES 2

3 egg whites

2 eggs

6 cherry tomatoes

1 bunch fresh spinach, leaves picked

½ cup (60g, 2oz) Parmesan cheese, grated

1½ tsps fresh basil, chopped (or 1tsp dried basil)

⅛ tsp salt

¼ tsp freshly ground black pepper

½ tbsp olive oil, for frying

Preheat grill to a medium setting.

Whisk egg whites and eggs together in a medium bowl and stir through whole tomatoes, spinach, cheese, basil, salt and black pepper

Heat oil in a frying pan over medium heat. Add the mixture and cook, covered, for 3 minutes or until almost set.

Remove from heat and place under grill for 2 minutes or until egg is set. Slice into four pieces and serve.

TOMATOES

The best thing to do with tomatoes is to not overthink, as a fresh tomato is a beautiful thing. Cherry tomatoes are bite size, juicy and burst in the mouth. Better than a lollipop. Roma tomatoes are almost buttery and can be happily shared. And heirloom tomatoes, which are the vine-ripened beauties sold at farmer's markets and in local vegetable shops, have so many shapes and flavours, the salad bowl could inspire a game of 'guess the tomato'. Chop up a medley of all of these and there's not even a need for a dressing.

Eggs Baked in Avocado Boats

ALL ABOARD! RICH AND SATISFYING, THIS COLOURFUL AND ENERGISING DISH IS QUICK TO MAKE AND EAT

SERVES 2

1 large avocado, halved and stone removed

¼ tsp ground cumin

2 eggs

Salt and ground black pepper, to taste

1 tbsp red capsicum, finely chopped

1 spring onion, finely sliced

2 slices fresh lime

Preheat oven to 220°C (430°F, Gas Mark 7).

Halve the avocado and remove the seed. Depending on the size of your avocado seed, you may need to make the make the holes larger. You need them to be big enough to fit the eggs.

Place avocado halves in separate ramekins or gently nestled together in a small baking dish. You need them to sit flat so that the eggs don't run out of the holes. Sprinkle a pinch of the cumin into each hole, then crack 1 egg into each avocado half. Season with salt, black pepper, and any other seasonings you like.

Bake in the oven until egg is cooked through or how you like it, around 12 minutes.

Remove from oven and sprinkle over the capsicum and spring onion.

Squeeze over some fresh lime to taste.

CHIA

Chia is a graceful little seed, with the power to transform a sleepy day into a productive one.

Their super quality is energy that lasts for hours. Forget sports drinks with sugar and artificial ingredients. Chia seeds are the 'it' seeds these days as foodies and nutritionists have finally clued into ancient wisdom: 'chia' is reportedly the Mayan word for strength. These chewy drops were an essential energy source for the Mayans and the Aztecs way back in 1500BC, who ate and drank chia to keep them going through hot days and long nights.

And what the Mayans knew, research has now confirmed. Chia seeds are a source of stable energy as they are made of equal parts protein, fats and fibre. Unlike jelly babies and caffeine, the rush will last. They won't cause spikes and drops in blood sugar or insulin levels, so that 11am craving for … something … will be so yesterday.

HOW TO BUY, PREPARE AND STORE CHIA SEEDS

- The dry seeds can be bought in packets at health-food stores and in the health-food aisles of most supermarkets.
- If you can afford it, opt for organic brands, and it's best to look out for the non-GMO label, to avoid added processing that can interfere with the nutrient quality.
- Good-quality chia seeds are naturally black or white or a speckled combination of these two colours. They shouldn't be brown.
- If adding to dishes that have liquid, just add dry and be ready for them to expand — in porridge, yoghurt, juice or soups.
- Look out for the term 'chia egg', a reference to chia's ability to replace an egg in cooking. Easy to make, you simply soak chia seeds in water in a ratio of 1:3 (chia to water) and place in the fridge for 15 minutes.
- If adding to salads or pastas with not much sauce, soak the seeds first in cool water for a few hours or overnight.
- Chia seeds are super sustainable and will keep for several years when stored in a cool, dry place.

A SIMPLE BREAKFAST PUDDING

Mix ¼ cup of chia seeds in 1 cup of liquid — almond milk and fruit juice are the healthiest of choices. Once the seeds have gelled up and the mixture is no longer watery, the 'pudding' is ready to eat. For more flavour, add cinnamon, honey, chopped fruit or nuts. This can take as little as 15 minutes and the pudding keeps for several days in the fridge. So many pluses.

Overnight Choc Chia Pudding

SERVES 2

1 cup (250ml, 8fl oz) almond milk

3 tbsps chia seeds

1 tsp vanilla extract

1½ tbsps cacao powder

2 tsps maple syrup

Shredded coconut, to garnish

Dark chocolate chips, to garnish

Chia seeds, to garnish

Place the almond milk, chia seeds, vanilla extract and cacao into a jar with a sealable lid. Tighten the lid and shake until nicely mixed up.

Transfer to the fridge to soak overnight or for a minimum of 8 hours.

When ready to serve, stir in the maple syrup and spoon into jars. Top with shredded coconut, dark chocolate chips and a few chia seeds.

Mango Chia Cups

SERVES 2

1 cup (250ml, 8fl oz) coconut milk

3 tbsps chia seeds

2 tbsps honey or maple syrup

½ tsp vanilla extract

½ mango, pureed

4 tbsps coconut yoghurt

4 tbsps toasted muesli

Fresh fruit and mint leaves, to garnish

In a jar or mixing bowl, combine coconut milk, chia seeds, honey or syrup and vanilla.

Cover with plastic wrap and chill in fridge for 15 minutes to allow chia to absorb and swell.

Remove and stir to thoroughly combine then return to the fridge for at least 2 hours.

Remove from fridge and layer half of the mango puree, chia mixture, coconut yoghurt and muesli in each serving glass.

Garnish with mint leaves and fruit of your choice.

COCONUT

Was there ever a more appealing symbol of summer and freedom? Summer and freedom on a distant island! Coconuts are full of potassium, fibre and healthy fats, a fact that has been researched lately — this hearty fruit was once thought to contribute to cholesterol levels and is now believed to reduce it. The health benefits of coconuts are now embraced by athletes and anyone who wants to move. On an island, climb a tree and start drinking. At home, instead of a fizzy drink for lunch, grab a coconut water, which has become the hydrating energy drink of choice.

Buckwheat Porridge with Maple Yoghurt and Plum Puree

AN IDEAL WINTERTIME WARMER THAT'S NUTRITIOUS, TASTY AND COMFORTINGLY WHOLESOME TOO

SERVES 2

PORRIDGE

200g (7oz) buckwheat groats

1 tsp of cinnamon

¼ tsp vanilla extract

1 cup (230ml, 8fl oz) water

2 cups (500ml, 1pt) milk

PUREE

2 cups (400g, 14oz) plums, halved and stoned

¾ cup (165g, 6oz) sugar

1 tsp cinnamon

1 tsp lemon rind

1 tbsp orange juice

MAPLE YOGHURT

2 tbsps maple syrup

2 cups (450g, 1lb) plain yoghurt

4 tbsps cashew butter (optional)

¼ cup (30g, 1oz) walnuts, whole

Mint leaves, to garnish

PORRIDGE

Start by placing your buckwheat groats in a medium bowl and soak them in lots of water overnight. In the morning, drain and rinse them.

Put them in a medium saucepan as well as the cinnamon, vanilla and water. Bring to the boil then reduce the heat and cover with a lid. As the water starts to be absorbed, add half the milk and stir it in.

Cover the groats and allow them to simmer gently, stirring frequently to ensure the porridge doesn't stick.

Once more of the liquid is absorbed, add the remaining milk and keep gently cooking until the porridge is at a consistency you like. This whole process can take up to half an hour. The longer it cooks the more digestible and softer the groats will be. If you want to go over the 30-minute mark, just make sure you add more liquid as needed.

PUREE

In a small saucepan over medium heat, cook the plums, sugar, cinnamon, lemon rind and orange juice for 10 minutes or until the plums are falling apart. You shouldn't need any more liquid but if it's looking a bit dry at first, add another tablespoon of orange juice. Remove the mixture from the saucepan.

Using an immersion blender, puree the plum mix until smooth then set aside to cool.

In a small bowl add the maple syrup to the yoghurt and stir well to combine.

Layer porridge, yoghurt and puree in glass serving jars. If using, place 1 tablespoon of cashew butter on top and garnish with sliced walnuts and mint.

Blueberry Chia Jam

THIS BRIGHT AND GORGEOUS JAM IS SUPREMELY SIMPLE TO MAKE AND CONTAINS A SECRET SUPERSEED

SERVES 6

1¼ cups (125g, 4½ oz) fresh blueberries

1 tsp lemon juice

1 tbsp pure maple syrup

2 tbsps chia seeds

In a small saucepan, add 1 cup of the blueberries, lemon juice and maple syrup and bring to a simmer or until the mixture begins to bubble and break down.

Remove the mixture from the heat and let it cool.

Using a blender, whiz the mix until reasonably well combined. Then remove to a bowl.

Add the chia seeds and the rest of the blueberries and stir thoroughly. Make sure there are no chia seeds that have clumped together.

Let the mixture sit for a couple of hours so that is has completely thickened into a jam.

Store in an airtight glass container and it will keep for 1 week.

Breakfast Quinoa Bowl

A FRESH CONTEMPORARY TWIST ON THE PORRIDGE BOWL THAT'S FULL OF NUTRIENTS AND FOOD FOR FUEL

SERVES 1

1 cup (170g, 6oz) red quinoa

2 cups (500ml, 1pt) coconut milk

2 tbsps maple syrup

1 small pinch sea salt

¾ tsp cinnamon

¼ tsp vanilla extract

¼ cup (30g, 1oz) walnuts, lightly toasted and chopped

Blueberries and banana, to serve

Milk, to serve

Bring the quinoa, coconut milk, maple syrup and salt to the boil in a medium-sized saucepan over a medium-high heat. Reduce to a simmer and cook, stirring frequently, for 10 minutes or until quinoa has absorbed all the moisture and is light and fluffy. Add more liquid if needed during cooking to achieve the right consistency. Stir in the cinnamon and vanilla extract.

To serve, top with the nuts, fruit and milk.

Fruit Salad with Couscous

COUSCOUS FOR BREAKFAST — WHY NOT? ITS BUTTERY GOODNESS IS THE PERFECT COMPANION TO SWEET, BRIGHT FRUIT

SERVES 4

1½ cups (375ml, 13fl oz) water

3 tbsps olive oil

1 cup (190g, 7oz) couscous

2 tbsps orange juice

1 tbsp apple cider vinegar

Pinch salt and pepper

8 small basil leaves

2 yellow nectarines, chopped

2 apricots, chopped

2 kiwi fruit, chopped

1½ cups (185g, 6oz) fresh raspberries

COUSCOUS

Bring the water to a boil in a medium saucepan. Add 1 tablespoon of the olive oil and the couscous. Stir once to mix up the couscous. Remove from the heat and cover with a lid.

The couscous should take about 10 minutes to soak up all the water. If it's still a little crunchy, put the lid back on and let it sit another couple of minutes.

Use a fork to stir it up, this helps separate the grains and make it fluffy. Put aside to cool.

SALAD

In a large bowl, whisk the remaining oil, orange juice, vinegar, salt and pepper. Gently mix through the basil, couscous, nectarines, apricots, kiwi fruit and raspberries.

Savoury Porridge with Mushrooms

EARTHY, SALTY, HEARTY, THIS SAVOURY PORRIDGE IS SURE TO MAKE YOU FEEL WARM AND FUZZY ALL DAY LONG

SERVES 4

1 cup (90g, 3oz) quick oats

1-2 tsps olive oil

1 clove garlic, crushed

250g (8oz) button mushrooms, sliced

4 sprigs fresh thyme, chopped

1 tsp salt

1 handful fresh baby spinach, stems removed, leaves chopped

2 tsps white miso

3 tbsps soy sauce

4 eggs

Cook the oats as directed on the package.

While the oats cook, heat the oil in a medium-large frying pan over medium heat. Add the garlic, mushrooms, thyme and salt. Cook the mushrooms for about 6 minutes, stirring frequently until they are browned. Add the spinach, cover the frying pan and let it all cook for 1 minute. You want the spinach to be slightly wilted, not thoroughly cooked or soggy. Remove from the heat.

Whisk together 2 tablespoons of hot water, along with the miso and soy sauce. Stir this mixture into the cooked porridge.

In a separate, non-stick, large frying pan add a dash of olive oil and fry all four eggs until they are how you like them. Divide the porridge into serving bowls. Top each bowl with the vegetables and a fried egg and serve.

Sardines on Rye with Herbs

SERVES 4

150g (5½ oz) cream cheese

8 slices rye bread

2 tbsps (15g, ½ oz) dill, roughly chopped

¼ cup (10g, ¼ oz) loosely packed parsley, roughly chopped

2 x 120g (4oz) cans sardines in olive oil, drained

Cracked pepper, to taste

1 lemon, cut into 8 slices

Divide the cream cheese evenly between the 8 slices of rye, spreading it evenly over each slice.

Again, divide the dill and parsley evenly between the slices, heaping it evenly on top of the cream cheese.

Halve the sardines lengthways, then place them, skin side up, on top of the herbs and cheese.

Sprinkle some freshly cracked pepper over each slice.

Serve with a slice of lemon on the side.

Buckwheat with Mushrooms

SERVES 2

1 cup (250ml, 8fl oz) warm vegetable stock

½ cup (90g, 3oz) roasted buckwheat (kasha), well rinsed

1½ tbsps olive oil

1 small onion, finely chopped

2 cloves garlic, crushed

250g (8oz) button mushrooms, sliced

2 tbsps lemon juice

1 tbsp dill, chopped

Salt and pepper, to taste

Bring the vegetable stock to a boil and add buckwheat. Cover and reduce heat to low. Cook for 25 minutes or until the buckwheat has cooked through. The buckwheat should be chewy but not so it's an effort to eat.

Heat the olive oil in a large saucepan. Add onion and garlic and cook gently, stirring, for 5 minutes, until soft. Turn the heat up to medium-high and add the sliced mushrooms to the pan. Cook until mushrooms are tender.

Add lemon juice and dill to the pan and combine well. Add cooked buckwheat and season to taste salt and pepper. Cook for a few minutes until warm, then serve.

PROTEIN

Protein, protein, protein. It sometimes seems that the world is obsessed with protein. There are diets that suggest protein is king — or queen. Or king and queen. And it's true that protein is what helps bodies get up in the morning and move during the day, let alone take up a new sport or a dance lesson.

Yet, it's not all about big muscles and perfect torsos. Protein is the essential building block to keep bodies strong and hearts beating. The heart is a muscle and it needs protein for strength and lubrication. And after any workout, whether it's a long walk on the beach or a long day at work, protein is what allows muscles to repair.

To get specific, for most, a daily dose of around 1g of protein per 1kg of body weight is recommended. Athletes and mover-shakers are recommended about 1.4g per 1kg of body weight daily. After exercise, protein is particularly important since muscles are most ready to absorb its fuel.

A lot of the hype about high-protein diets comes along with recommendations for protein powders, shakes and bars, which deliver the stuff in quick, easy bites and guzzles. These are all fine on occasion and for convenience and some of them are quite enjoyable. However, there is protein in most foods and it's far better to take in nutrients through natural ingredients than through processed foods.

PROTEIN IN THE SIMPLEST, DAILY FOODS

EGGS: There are about 6g of protein in a mid-sized egg, which is about 6% of a daily protein requirement. For one egg!

MILK: The cup of milk before bed is not just for restless children. Sip one slowly, perhaps warmed to aid sleep, and set the amino acids in milk's protein to work as the body rests.

YOGHURT: A cup of Greek yoghurt has about 6g of protein, which is whopping for such a small portion. Try to resist flavoured yoghurts that are crammed with sugar. Better to DIY toppings like honey, dark chocolate, nuts or a few dried apricots.

GREEN PEAS: Frozen or fresh, a cup of green peas has just a touch more protein than one egg in it. Green pea omelette, anyone? Add Swiss or Parmesan cheese and get ready for a night of completely focused study … or much more fun, a twilight jog.

FISH AND SEAFOOD: Red meat is the obvious protein machine, yet the fruits of the sea are sometimes overlooked as sources of energy. Tuna and salmon are bursting with protein and amino acids and the omega-3 helps tired joints mellow out after a workout. A small tin of tuna has as much protein as a 3-egg omelette.

Farmer's Breakfast

A PERFECT WINTER COMFORT BREAKFAST THAT WILL GET YOU MOVING AND KEEP YOU GOING THROUGH THE MORNING

SERVES 4

1½ tbsps olive oil

1 brown onion, finely chopped

350g (12oz) thick bacon, cut into pieces

150g (5oz) potatoes (kipfler or another waxy variety for frying), diced

1 yellow capsicum, chopped (red will do, if yellow unavailable)

1 tsp ground cumin

1 tsp sweet paprika

3 eggs

¼ cup (30g, 1oz) tasty cheese, grated

Fresh parsley, chopped, to garnish

Heat the oil in a large frying pan over medium heat. Add the onion and bacon and cook for 5 minutes, until the bacon is crisp.

Add the potatoes, capsicum, cumin and paprika and fry, stirring regularly for 10 minutes or until the potatoes are golden brown. Remove the potato mixture from the pan and put aside.

Gently break eggs into the pan. Return the potato mix to the pan, placing it carefully around the eggs.

Sprinkle the cheese over the top, around the eggs, and cook on med-high for 1 minute or until the eggs are cooked the way you prefer them.

Season with salt and pepper, garnish eith chopped parsley, and serve.

Home-Made Baked Beans

A HIGH-PROTEIN, LOW-SUGAR OPTION — JUST THE WAY BAKED BEANS SHOULD BE

SERVES 2-4

1 tbsp olive oil

1 onion, chopped

1kg (2 lbs) Roma tomatoes, chopped

¼ cup (60g, 2oz) passata or tomato puree

1 carrot, sliced

2 x 400g (14oz) cans borlotti beans

Pinch of sea salt

1 tbsp maple syrup

1 tbsp butter

Fresh basil leaves, to garnish

Heat the oil in a large saucepan over a medium-high heat. Add the onion and saute for 6-8 minutes, or until soft and translucent.

Add the chopped tomatoes, passata or tomato puree and carrot and stir to combine.

Cover and reduce heat to medium low and cook at a gentle simmer for 10 minutes, until a thick tomato sauce has formed and the carrot has softened.

Add beans, salt and maple syrup and cook for a further 5 minutes until the beans have heated through.

Add the butter and mix through until melted and shiny. Garnish with fresh basil leaves.

Serve as a main or accompaniment to poached eggs.

Scrambled Tofu with Mushrooms

GET TODAY OFF TO A GREAT START WITH PROTEIN-PACKED TOFU, NUTRIENT-BOOSTING SPINACH AND MINERAL-RICH MUSHROOMS

SERVES 2

Olive oil, for frying

¼ onion, finely chopped

6 button mushrooms, sliced

225g (8oz, ½ lb) silken tofu

1 bunch spinach, chopped, stalks removed

Handful of basil, torn

Heat the oil in a frying pan over a medium heat and saute onion and mushrooms for 5-6 minutes, until the mushrooms are tender and browning at the edges and the onion is translucent.

Add the tofu to the frying pan and stir well to scramble, leaving some larger chunks and breaking the rest of the tofu down to a 'scrambled egg' consistency.

Add spinach and basil and stir through.

Stir-fry tofu mix for 3 minutes until thoroughly heated through.

Chorizo Breakfast Burrito

BURSTING WITH ZESTY FLAVOURS, YOU CAN EAT THIS PROTEIN-PACKED BURRITO ON THE GO

SERVES 1

½ tbsp olive oil

1 small potato (kipfler or waxy variety), chopped into small cubes

1 chorizo, chopped into small cubes

1 large egg, beaten

1 tbsp spring onions, sliced

1 x 15cm (6 inch) flour tortilla

1 tbsp tasty cheese, grated

½ tbsp fresh coriander, chopped

1 tsp chilli sauce or salsa

1 tbsp Greek yoghurt

1 wedge fresh lime

In a small-medium frying pan, heat the oil to hot and add the potato and fry for 3 minutes.

Add the chorizo pieces and cook for a further 5 minutes until chorizo is fully cooked. Remove mix from pan and set aside.

Reduce the heat to low and add the egg and spring onions to the pan and roughly scramble the egg to the consistency you like. Remove from heat.

Along the centre of the tortilla, place the chorizo mix and the egg. Sprinkle over the cheese and coriander. Add the chilli sauce or salsa to taste, dollop over the yoghurt and give a squeeze of fresh lime juice.

Roll up the burrito and serve.

High-Energy Snacks

BUCKWHEAT

It turns out there is no wheat in buckwheat, which is just one reason it's such a wonder food. Call it the undercover agent of the seed world — crunchy and golden when hulled or buoyant and green when unhulled, the seed has had health nuts over the moon in recent years, due to its versatility. It can be whipped into pancakes and muffins or churned into pasta-like noodles and the only difference is in flavour — buckwheat slices, biscuits and bite-size energy morsels tend to be nutty and subtly salty. The seed comes from a plant with broad leaves that is similar to rhubarb, that rich, red fruit with the hearty green leaves that is also lovely breakfast fare.

THE HEALTHY FACTS

Living adventurously is a lot more possible with energy and a well-oiled body. Buckwheat has a bunch of powerful natural characteristics. It has more protein than rice, wheat, millet or corn and protein leads to that happy state of being full of beans. Laziness can set in when there is literally not enough fuel to inspire a day surfing waves or hiking up a mountain.

The protein in buckwheat is pumping with amino acids — lysine and arginine, to be specific, which are excellent on their own and also have a chemical effect when mixed in with beans and certain cereals. Buckwheat actually boosts the protein value of beans and grains when they are stewed up together or hand-rolled together into a veggie burger. So pancakes and waffles that are made of buckwheat might inspire a morning run rather than a mid-morning nap. Buckwheat is also thought to lower cholesterol and reduce and stabilise blood sugar levels, which is helpful in the prevention of diabetes and obesity. This means: pancakes for breakfast no longer need be a rare special occasion.

BUCKWHEAT ACROSS THE WORLD

Like wheat and corn in the Western world, buckwheat kernels are a staple food in Eastern Europe. Hulled buckwheat kernels are called groats and most commonly eaten there as a creamy porridge for breakfast or flavoured with a stock of onions, olive oil and fresh parsley and turned into a stew.

In China, Korea and Japan, buckwheat has been cultivated and turned into noodles and dumpling cases for at least a thousand years. In Japanese restaurants, soba noodles are the spaghetti of the menu. The texture is lighter and grainier than spaghetti and all they need is a splash of soy sauce or to be stirred with a bunch of shitake mushrooms and seaweed. In many countries, long noodles are a symbol of longevity, and are eaten across Asia on New Year's Day.

Buckwheat Energy Bar

THESE CHEWY, SWEET SNACKS ARE THE PERFECT HEALTHY ENERGY BOOSTERS FOR ACTIVE LIVES

SERVES 4

½ cup (90g, 3oz) dates, chopped

¼ cup (50g, 2 oz) dried apricots, chopped

1½ cups (275g, 9oz) buckwheat groats

¼ cup (30g, 1oz) raw cacao powder

½ tsp vanilla extract

¼ tsp salt

2 heaped tbsps coconut oil

¼ tsp cinnamon

¼ tsp ground cardamom

Soak the dates and apricots in enough warm water to cover them for about 20 minutes until they soften.

Remove the fruit from the water and set aside but save the water in case you need some of the liquid.

In a blender, mix together all the remaining ingredients except the buckwheat until you have a smooth paste.

In a large bowl stir together the fruit, buckwheat and blended ingredients until everything is thoroughly mixed. Add the fruit water as needed if it's too thick to stir.

Scoop out mixture into an 18 x 28 cm (7 x 11in) slice tin lined with baking paper and flatten down with a spatula or the back of a spoon.

Chill in the freezer for at least 30 minutes for the mixture to firm.

Cut into slices of your preferred size.

Store in an airtight container and it will keep for at least 2 weeks.

Buckwheat Salmon Patties

A GREAT HEALTHY SNACK WITH MINIMUM FUSS REQUIRED IN THE KITCHEN

SERVES 2

400g (14oz) fresh salmon (if using canned, use pink salmon)

1 egg, beaten

¼ cup (40 g, 1oz) leek, finely chopped — white part only

½ cup (60g, 2oz) buckwheat flour

¼ cup (20g, ¾ oz) cannellini beans, mashed.

Pinch salt and black pepper

¼ tsp of ground cumin

¼ tsp ground cayenne pepper

Olive oil

Parsley, to garnish

If using salmon from cans, drain the liquid in a separate small bowl and set aside. If using fresh salmon, remove the skin.

In a medium bowl, add the salmon, egg, leek, flour, beans, salt, pepper and spices. Stir well until thoroughly mixed. If needed, use your hands. If needed, add some of the can liquid or water to get it to a thick mashed consistency.

Divide the mixture into 8 portions and fashion them into patties.

In a medium frying pan, heat the olive oil on medium-high heat.

Fry the patties, squashing them down slightly, for 5 minutes on each side, or until golden brown and cooked through.

Serve with parsley as a garnish.

Apricot Almond Balls

MAKES 12

1 cup (190g, 7oz) dried apricots

½ cup (85g, 3oz) pitted dates

1 cup (125g, 4oz) raw almonds

1 tbsp chia seeds

½ cup (40g, 1½ oz) shredded coconut

½ tsp vanilla extract

Pinch of salt

Place all of the ingredients in a high-speed blender or food processor.

Process until the ingredients are fully combined and the mixture holds together when pressed. Process for longer to achieve a finer consistency.

Using damp hands, roll the mixture into balls of the desired size.

Transfer to the fridge to chill until ready to eat.

NOTE: Will keep in the fridge for up to 4 weeks.

Apricot Yoghurt Muffins

MAKES 12

1 cup (125g, 4oz) wholemeal flour

1 cup (125g, 4oz) plain flour

1½ tsps baking powder

1 tsp cinnamon

½ tsp ground cardamom

⅔ cup (100g, 3oz) raw sugar

1 cup (190g, 7oz) dried apricots, chopped into quarters

1 egg, lightly beaten

5 tbsps butter, melted and cooled slightly

1 cup (250ml, 8fl oz) Greek yoghurt

½ tsp vanilla extract

Preheat oven to 190°C (375°F, Gas Mark 5). Grease a muffin tin or line with paper cups.

In a large bowl, sift the flours, baking powder, cinnamon and cardamom. Add the sugar and apricots and stir gently to combine. Make a well in your mixture. In a separate bowl, mix together the egg, butter, yoghurt and vanilla. Add the egg mix to the flour and roughly mix using a large spoon or a flat spatula. Spoon the mixture into the muffin tin. Bake in the oven for 20 minutes.

DRIED APRICOTS

Eating just one of these chewy beauties can satisfy cravings for less healthy sweets. They are full of fibre and excellent for dosing up on potassium and vitamin A for eyes that see in the night time. The trick is to find the brands that don't add sugar or, ideally, sulphites, which are added as a preservative to most dried fruits. Sulphites are limited by the Australian government. Still, it's best to stick to organic brands and then go all out adding these sweet morsels to muesli, salads and baked treats.

Nutty Apricot Granola Bars

PACKED WITH THE GOODNESS OF SEEDS, NUTS AND DRIED FRUIT, THESE BARS ARE GREAT FOR A POST WORKOUT PICK-ME-UP

SERVES 8

2 cups (180g, 6oz) rolled oats

½ cup (70g, 2½ oz) raw sunflower seeds

¾ cup (95g, 3oz) pepitas (pumpkin seeds)

1 cup (125g, 4oz) sliced almonds

¼ cup (35g, 1¼ oz) flaxseed

½ cup (180g, 6oz) maple syrup

¼ cup (40g, 1½ oz) packed brown sugar

3 tbsps unsalted butter

2 tsps vanilla extract

½ tsp salt

½ cup (85g, 3oz) dried apricots, chopped

¼ cup (30g, 1oz) dried cranberries, chopped

¼ cup (25g, 1oz) dessicated coconut

Line an 18 x 28cm (7 x 11in) slice tin with baking paper and set aside. Preheat the oven to 180°C (350°F, Gas Mark 4).

Spread the oats, sunflower seeds, pepitas, almonds, and flaxseed onto a large flat baking tray. Place in the oven and toast for 10-15 minutes, stirring every 5 minutes. Once toasted set aside to cool.

In a large saucepan over medium heat, mix the maple syrup, brown sugar, butter, vanilla and salt. Gently stir until the sugar has completely dissolved, then remove from the heat.

Add the toasted mix, dried fruit and coconut and stir to combine thoroughly.

Spoon out the mixture into the tin and and press down firmly to make sure the mixture is evenly distributed.

Bake for 20 minutes until the edges and top are a very light golden brown. Cut the bars into your desired shapes but leave them in the pan to cool to room temperature before taking them out.

NOTE: These bars can be stored in an airtight container in the fridge for up to 2 weeks.

DARK CHOCOLATE

For years, the health experts warned off chocolate, one of the food world's most addictive and accessible treats. When studies started emerging that it was actually doing good, life became a lot more fun.

Imagine climbing a mountain without a bag of scroggin (trail mix) for snack stops. Or imagine Easter without at least a chocolate egg. There is solid research backing the inclusion of dark chocolate in all activities — solo, meditative, romantic and marathon-like. Eating one square of dark chocolate during the afternoon slump at the office has the same boost on energy as a macchiato or short black and that energy lasts longer, plus is packed with nutrients. When day turns to night, sharing a dark chocolate molten cake with the sweetie after a candlelit dinner will stave off a food coma, so a midnight stroll up to the local lookout won't seem like an outlandish adventure.

Imagine packing a treat such as pistachio, apricot and dark chocolate energy bars or sea salt and dark chocolate detox balls into a picnic basket and letting the GPS lead the way to an unknown spot for a Sunday out. Or inviting your friends on a hike with the caveat that everyone bring a snack containing dark chocolate. It would be an original idea, it will be a delicious day and will also ensure that the hike doesn't end at lunch time with a group laze about.

The thing with dark chocolate is that, unlike milk chocolate, which will make you fall asleep in the sun, the cocoa goes to work and will actually make the legs bounce.

How does it do this? It has to do with the very crafty workings of our organs and with metabolism: the cocoa in dark chocolate is less processed than milk chocolate and, weirdly, has been found to be largely indigestible. This is weird because it's a good thing. There is a chemical process that is stimulated when the cocoa just sits there that has been linked to a lower risk of heart disease. The gut bacteria creates metabolites, which the bloodstream drinks up and this essentially cools the heart down. Kind of like a cool shower or a quick dip for the heart.

In case you find the thought challenging, here are a few ideas for switching from milk to dark:

- Switch milk chocolate for dark chocolate in the creamy, fluffy mousse at dinner parties.
- Get the dark chocolate souffle rising — an impressive dish to serve.
- Put dark chocolate chips in the biscuits — they are saltier and chunkier than milk chocolate.
- Heat up a dark chocolate sauce to drizzle over buckwheat pancakes for breakfast or a dessert.
- Try a dark chocolate, flourless chocolate cake that is gluten free and light on the heart and belly.

Peanut Butter Coffee Brownies

THESE DECADENT BROWNIES WILL KEEP THE WHOLE SOCCER OR NETBALL TEAM POWERING THROUGH THE SECOND HALF

MAKES 9

250g (9oz) unsalted butter

1 cup (160g, 6oz) milk chocolate chips

100g (3½ oz) dark chocolate, chopped

2 tbsps cocoa powder

1 cup (220g, 8oz) plus 2 tbsps raw sugar

3 large eggs

1½ tbsps instant coffee

1 tbsp vanilla extract

⅔ cup (80g, 3oz) plain flour

1½ tsps baking powder

½ tsp salt

250g (9oz) crunchy peanut butter

½ cup (60g, 2oz) salted peanuts, chopped

Preheat oven to 180°C (350°F, Gas Mark 4). Line an 18 x 28cm (7 x 11in) slice tin with baking paper and lightly grease with melted butter.

In a medium saucepan over low heat, add the butter, chocolates and cocoa powder. Gently stir until the chocolate is melted and smooth. Remove from heat.

In a large bowl, roughly mix the sugar, eggs, coffee and vanilla. Add the warm chocolate mixture and stir to combine. Set aside to cool down to room temperature.

In a medium bowl, sift the flour, baking powder and salt. Add this to the chocolate mixture, a third at a time to ensure it's mixed in thoroughly. Mix through the peanut butter and peanuts.

Pour your mix into the prepared tin and spread around evenly. Bake for 35 minutes (do not overbake). A skewer inserted should come out mostly clean but with a some melted chocolate on it. You want them nice and gooey but not unmanageable. Cool completely to room temperature before cutting into desired shapes.

Peanut Caramel Chocolate Bars

THESE NO-BAKE, NO-FUSS SNACKS ARE AN IDEAL PICK-ME-UP READY TO INDULGE IN WHEN YOU NEED IT MOST

SERVES 6-8

225g (8oz, ½ lb) milk chocolate, chopped

¾ cup (165g, 6oz) sugar

¼ cup (60ml, 2fl oz) water

⅓ cup (80ml, 3fl oz) heavy cream, at room temperature

170g (6oz) white chocolate, chopped

1 tsp sea salt

1 cup (125g, 4oz) salted peanuts, divided

Grease and line the bottom and sides of a shallow baking tin.

Place milk chocolate in a small heatproof bowl set over simmering water, and stir until just melted. Turn off heat.

Combine sugar and water in a large saucepan over a low heat and cook, stirring occasionally, until sugar has dissolved. Increase heat to high and allow the mixture to bubble for 5 minutes, or until the syrup begins to golden at the edges. Don't stir during this time. Swirl pan over the heat until the mixture is an even colour and then cook undisturbed for a further 3 minutes, or until the syrup turns a 'treacle colour'.

Remove from the heat and slowly add the cream, being mindful of any hot splashes. Stir until well combined. Add white chocolate and salt and stir until melted and mixture is smooth. Add half the peanuts and stir again to combine. Set aside for 5 minutes to cool slightly.

Pour the peanut mixture into the prepared tin over the milk chocolate and spread it evenly. Freeze for 45 minutes, or until cold and firm.

Remove from freezer. Reheat the milk chocolate, if needed to make it pourable, and pour it over the caramel. Spread evenly with a spatula. Sprinkle with remaining peanuts. Refrigerate for 30 minutes, until very cold before slicing.

Chocolate Gingerbread Cake

A CLASSIC CHOCOLATE CAKE WITH A ZINGY GINGER KICK THAT WILL POWER YOU THROUGH THE AFTERNOON

SERVES 4

2¼ cups (280g, 9oz) plain flour

¼ cup (30g, 1oz) unsweetened cocoa powder

2 tsps baking powder

½ tsp salt

1 tsp cinnamon

1 tsp ground cardamom

1 tsp ground cloves

¼ tsp nutmeg

½ tsp ground black pepper

¼ cup (40g, 1½ oz) brown sugar

120g (4oz) unsalted butter, softened

2 tbsps fresh ginger, finely grated

2 eggs (room temperature)

1 cup (350g, 12oz) molasses

220g (8oz) dark cooking chocolate, melted

½ cup (125ml, 4fl oz) milk

½ cup (125ml, 4fl oz) hot water

CHOCOLATE GANACHE

220g (8oz) cooking chocolate, chopped

½ cup (125ml, 4fl oz) thickened cream

Preheat the oven to 190°C (375°F, Gas Mark 5). Grease a 23cm (9in) springform cake tin, then lightly dust it with flour.

In a large bowl, sift together the flour, cocoa, baking powder, salt, cinnamon, cardamom, cloves, nutmeg and pepper.

Using an electric mixer, mix together the brown sugar, butter and ginger until light and fluffy. Add the eggs, one at a time, ensuring both are thoroughly mixed through.

Add the molasses and melted chocolate to the mixing bowl, mix well to combine thoroughly. To this mixture, add the flour, milk and hot water in small amounts alternately, then mixing through to ensure the mixture isn't lumpy.

Pour the cake mix into the tin and bake for 40 minutes until a skewer inserted into the middle comes out clean. Once cooked, remove from tin and set aside to cool completely.

GANACHE

Heat a small heavy saucepan over low. Gently melt the chocolate and cream together. You need to mix them well, but try to do this with minimum stirring. The less you stir it, the silkier the ganache will look. Remove from the heat and set aside to cool slightly.

Gently pour the ganache over the top of the cake, let it cool slightly and serve.

ALMONDS

It's been almond mania in recent years, with bowls of almonds replacing bowls of peanuts for the ultimate finger food on top of bars and at the great summer barbecue. Perhaps this has been inspired by research showing the great things almonds do for the cardiovascular system. They are full of monounsaturated fats as well as vitamin E, fibre and a handful of potent antioxidants. Nuts in general contain fat, fibre and protein, a turbo-charged combo that can fuel a whole day of adventure even if there are no meals prepared. Take a ziplock bag of almonds on a long, meandering bike ride and even if the GPS gets lost, hunger won't be the issue.

THE LOW-DOWN

Nut allergies are common. Also, almonds are a member of the peach family — look at a peach pip next time and see the resemblance. And, like stone fruit, they can cause allergies in some people. Ever feel a little itch on the lips after a handful of almonds? Probably best to leave them alone or eat just a couple, which will give the benefits without the discomfort.

There's an endless debate about the fat in nuts and here's the great news: almonds can actually help with weight loss when eaten in moderation. To that end, raw or dry roasted are the healthiest.

WHAT TO DO WITH ALMONDS

There are many more virtues to this hearty little nut and ideas for cooking with it:

ALMOND BUTTER: Try this savoury, grainy spread instead of margarine or butter on toast. It also makes a tasty substitute for peanut butter.

ALMOND MILK: Try it in coffee and tea for a change. It's lactose free for those with sensitive stomachs. And making it at home is cheaper and quite simple: you just need water, a food processor and a sweetener. (And almonds!)

ALMOND OIL: A healthy oil for baking cakes and biscuits. More flavourful and much lighter on the heart than vegetable oil.

ALMOND CAKE: It can be so healthy, it's barely cake. Flourless almond cake with lemon juice is gluten free and an excellent substitute for an energy bar.

ALMOND SOUP: It's like a protein smoothie: warm, salty and creamy. The most basic recipe is a beautiful blend of almonds, water, olive oil and quite a bit of garlic for a zesty flavour and a boost to the immune system. Some recipes include lemon, coriander and mint. Season with salt and pepper and scrape the bowl with a slice of whole wheat bread for an immediate energy rush. Yum.

Yoghurt and Banana Pops

MAKES 4

¾ cup (50g, 2oz) almonds, chopped

1 tsp honey

¼ tsp ground cardamom

¾ cup (170g, 6oz) Greek yoghurt

2 ripe but firm bananas, peeled and halved

4 wooden icy-pole sticks

Heat a small frying pan or saucepan to medium-high. Dry-cook the almonds for 3 minutes, stirring constantly or until they are just browned. Remove from the pan immediately and set aside to cool.

In a small bowl, thoroughly mix the honey and cardamom into the yoghurt.

Gently insert the sticks into the cut ends of the bananas. Line a large flat baking tray with baking paper.

Place the yoghurt onto a small plate and do the same with the almonds. Roll the bananas in spiced yoghurt to coat them. Then gently roll each yoghurt banana in the almonds to lightly coat. Sprinkle some on top while you roll. Place the bananas on the tray and place in the freezer for a minimum of 1 hour, but ideally overnight.

Banana Oat Muffins

MAKES 12

1¾ cups (215g, 7oz) plain or whole wheat flour

⅓ cup (30g, 1oz) cup oats

½ tsp baking powder

1 tsp bicarbonate of soda

½ tsp nutmeg

3 ripe bananas, mashed

¾ cup (165g, 6oz) caster sugar

1 egg

80g (3oz) butter, melted

12 raw almonds, chopped

Preheat oven to 180°C (350°F, Gas Mark 4) and line a 12-hole muffin tin with paper cases.

Sift together the flour, oats, baking powder, bicarb, and nutmeg in a medium mixing bowl. Set aside.

Combine mashed bananas, sugar, egg and melted butter in a large mixing bowl. Gradually fold in dry ingredient mix, and combine with a metal spoon until smooth. Spoon into paper cases, filling two-thirds full with batter. Top each muffin with chopped almonds. Bake for 20 minutes, or until a skewer comes out clean.

YOGHURT

Yoghurt is an excellent source of protein and calcium and the best 'fake' cream a health nut could hope for. Dollop it on curries, in salad dressings and onto a baked potato instead of sour cream. And the creamier the better. Greek yoghurt or even full fat plain yoghurt is the best choice. Also, get creative with flavourings. Store-bought flavoured yogurts are packed with sugar and the taste is rarely as delicious as the real thing. A bowl of passionfruit drizzled over Greek yoghurt, on the other hand, can be eaten three times a day. And then for dessert.

Banana Nut Loaf

A CLASSIC SNACK THAT'S EXCUSABLE PRE-WORKOUT AS BANANA MAY HELP CURB THOSE MUSCLE CRAMPS

SERVES 8

2 cups (250g, 8oz) self-raising flour

⅓ cup (50g, 2oz) brown sugar

1 tsp bicarbonate of soda

2 large ripe bananas

2 eggs, whisked

1 tsp vanilla essence

1 cup (250ml, 8fl oz) milk

½ cup (60g, 2oz) walnuts, coarsely chopped

½ cup (60g, 2oz) almonds, coarsely chopped

Preheat the oven to 180°C (350°F, Gas Mark 4). Line the base and sides of a loaf tin with greaseproof paper.

Sift the flour into a large mixing bowl. Add sugar and bicarb and stir thoroughly to combine.

In a medium bowl, mash bananas with a fork.

Add eggs, vanilla, milk, banana, walnuts and almonds to the flour mixture and gently fold until well combined. Spoon mixture into the lined tin.

Place in the oven and bake for 45 minutes or until a skewer inserted into the centre comes out clean.

Set aside to cool completely. Cut into slices to serve.

Raw Carrot Cake Bars

A GREAT SNACK THAT PROVIDES A BOOST OF ENERGY WHEN YOU NEED IT, WHETHER YOU'RE HIKING OR OUT FOR A SUNDAY STROLL

MAKES 10

1 cup (175g, 6oz) dates, pitted

1 cup (140g, 5oz) almonds

¼ cup (30g, 1oz) cashews, roughly chopped

½ cup (40g, 1½ oz) desiccated coconut

½ cup (40g, 1½ oz) rolled oats

2 tbsps sunflower seeds

1 cup (50g, 2oz) carrot, finely grated with excess water squeezed out

¼ cup (90g, 3oz) honey

1 tsp ground cinnamon

½ tsp nutmeg

¼ tsp ground cloves

1 tsp vanilla extract

Line an 18 x 28cm (7 x 11in) slice tin with baking paper and lightly oil the paper.

In a food processor or blender, blend the dates into a paste. Remove the paste and set aside. Add the nuts, coconut, oats and sunflower seeds to the blender and pulse several times to create a coarse meal.

Add the date paste back to the blender in chunks and pulse a couple of times to roughly mix through. Add the carrot, honey, spices and vanilla. Process until fully combined.

Firmly press the mix into the slice tin, then place in the fridge for a few hours or overnight.

Slice into small squares while the mix is still in the tin, then remove and then break the squares up.

NOTE: These can be kept frozen in an airtight container for 1 month.

Pumpkin Choc Chip Bars

THESE HEALTHY SNACK BARS ARE A GUILT-FREE AND COMFORTING TREAT TO HELP YOU THROUGH THE DAY

MAKES 16

3 cups (270g, 9oz) rolled oats, tightly packed

¼ cup (30g, 1oz) wholemeal plain flour

2 tsps baking powder

½ tsp bicarbonate of soda

¼ tsp salt

1 tsp cinnamon

1 tsp ground cardamom

¼ tsp ground cloves

1 cup (225g, 8oz) cooked and mashed pumpkin

½ cup (80g, 3oz) brown sugar

2 tsps vanilla extract

½ cup (125ml, 4fl oz) milk

1 large egg

½ cup (80g, 3oz) mini chocolate chips

1 cup (90g, 3oz) shredded coconut

Preheat oven to 180°C (350°F, Gas Mark 4). Line an 18 x 28 cm (7 x 11in) slice tin with baking paper and lightly oil the paper.

In a blender or food processor, blend the oats until they resemble a rough flour.

In a large bowl add 2½ cups of the oat flour. Mix through the wholemeal flour, baking powder, bicarb, salt and spices. Make a well in the centre then set aside.

In a medium bowl, stir together pumpkin, brown sugar, vanilla extract, milk and egg until the mix is smooth.

Add the pumpkin mix to the flour in the bowl and stir to combine, adding the rest of the oat flour.

Gently stir through the chocolate chips and half of the coconut. Pour the mix into the prepared pan. Sprinkle over the top the rest of the coconut.

Bake for 20 minutes or until a skewer inserted into the middle comes out clean. Once cooked, let it cool to room temperature. Remove from the pan and cut into bars.

Roasted Honey Cinnamon Chickpeas

EASY TO PREPARE AND JUST AS EASY TO EAT, THESE CRUNCHY MORSELS ARE A GREAT EVERYDAY SNACK

SERVES 4

1 x 400g (14oz) can chickpeas

2 tsps olive oil

1 tbsp honey

1 tsp cinnamon

1 tsp brown sugar

Pinch of nutmeg

Pinch of salt

Preheat oven to 190°C (375°F, Gas Mark 5).

Line a large flat baking tray with baking paper.

Drain and rinse the chickpeas. Dry with a paper towel or tea towel. Place them on a towel to dry off. You can peel off the skins if you want.

In a medium bowl, stir together the oil, honey, cinnamon, sugar, nutmeg and salt.

Add the chickpeas to the bowl and stir until all the chickpeas are coated in the honey mixture.

Spread the chickpeas on the tray in a single layer.

Bake for around 40 minutes or until the chickpeas are crunchy all the way through.

Store the chickpeas in an airtight container at room temperature.

Roasted Spicy Chickpeas

SERVES 2

1 x 400g (14oz) can chickpeas

1 tbsp olive oil

1 tsp cayenne pepper

1 tsp ground cumin

¼ tsp sweet paprika

½ tsp sea salt

Preheat oven to 200°C (400°F, Gas Mark 6)

Line a large flat baking tray with baking paper.

Drain and rinse the chickpeas and pat dry with a paper towel or tea towel. You can peel off the skins if you prefer.

In a medium bowl, thoroughly mix together the oil, spices and salt. Add the chickpeas and toss to coat the chickpeas in the mixture.

Arrange chickpeas on a baking sheet in a single layer.

Bake for around 30 minutes or until the chickpeas are crunchy all the way through.

Store the chickpeas in an airtight container at room temperature.

Chickpea Stuffed Sweet Potato

SERVES 2

2 medium-sized sweet potatoes

3 tbsps olive oil

1 small onion, finely chopped

1 clove garlic, crushed

1 tsp ground cumin

½ tsp cayenne pepper

½ tsp smoked paprika

1 x 400g (14oz) can chickpeas, drained and rinsed

¼ cup (30g, 1oz) mozzarella cheese, grated

Preheat oven to 190°C (375°F, Gas Mark 5). Wrap the sweet potatoes in foil and roast in oven for at least 50 minutes, then remove and cut each potato in half lengthways and scoop out flesh into a large bowl.

In a frying pan, heat olive oil to medium-high heat. Fry onion and garlic for 4 minutes, then add the spices and chickpeas. Cook for a further 2 minutes.

Place the chickpea mix in the bowl with the scooped-out sweet potato. Mix in mozzarella. Stuff sweet potato skins with the chickpea mixture and bake again for 15 minutes until the cheese is melted and slightly crisped. Serve drizzled with yoghurt and lemon juice.

CHICKPEAS

Straight from the can, chickpeas can be added to pretty much any dish and double its fibre and protein content. One cup and a half can give as much muscle strength as a small chicken breast. And no summer barbecue or wintry dinner gathering would be a party without chickpeas. People forget that the essential appetiser, hummus is a simple blend of these humble, beige legumes and just a few other ingredients: lemon, salt, pepper, garlic and tahini (a middle eastern sesame paste). Add sun-dried tomatoes, red capsicum, chilli and any number of seasonings according to your taste.

Sweet Potato Burgers

GREAT AS PART OF A HEALTHY WEEKEND LUNCH SPREAD, THESE PATTIES ARE FULL OF GOODNESS

SERVES 6

1 x 400g (14oz) can chickpeas, drained and rinsed

½ cup (40g, 1½ oz) rolled oats

1 tsp dried oregano

½ tsp cayenne

½ tsp salt

50ml (2fl oz) lemon juice

1 small sweet potato, grated

½ cup (25g, 1oz) carrot, grated

1 egg

3 cloves garlic, crushed

½ cup (20g, ¾ oz) fresh coriander, finely chopped

Preheat oven to 190°C (375°F, Gas Mark 5) and line a large baking tray with baking paper.

In a food processor, combine the chickpeas, oats, spices, salt and lemon juice. Pulse several times until the ingredients are all finely chopped into a mixture that just holds together.

Transfer the chickpea mix to a large bowl. Add the sweet potato, carrot, egg, garlic and coriander. Mix everything together until well combined.

Using your hands, divide the mixture evenly into 6 portions. Press each portion into a patty and place on the baking tray. Bake in the oven for 15 minutes, then carefully flip the patties over and cook for another 15 minutes.

Serve patties with a side of rocket or lettuce.

Black Bean and Sweet Potato Quesadilla

A QUICK AND EASY SNACK THAT WILL TEMPT YOUR TASTEBUDS WITH THE SPICY FLAVOURS OF MEXICO

SERVES 4

1 tbsp olive oil

1 large sweet potato, peeled and chopped into small cubes

¼ tsp cumin

¼ tsp paprika

¼ tsp cayenne

1 cup (60g, 2oz) black beans

1½ cups (60g, 2oz) tasty cheese, grated

¾ cup (185ml, 6fl oz) tomato salsa

8 flour tortillas

In a medium frying pan, heat the olive oil over medium-high heat. Add the sweet potatoes and spices and stir to coat the potato with the spices. Cover and cook for 10 minutes until the potatoes are softened.

Remove the potatoes from the pan and place into a large bowl. Allow to cool for 15 minutes.

Add the beans, cheese and salsa to the potatoes and mix thoroughly and gently, taking care not to mash the potato too much.

Spread the sweet potato mix over one half of each tortilla. Fold over the tortillas into halves.

Heat a large frying pan over medium heat. Fry the tortillas for 2-3 minutes on each side until they are browned all over and the cheese is melted.

Crispy Chickpea Fritters

GET A FIBRE AND ENERGY BOOST WITH THIS FILLING
SNACK THAT WILL KEEP YOU GOING THROUGH THE DAY

SERVES 2

1 cup (200g 7oz) dried
chickpeas

1 tsp cumin seeds

1 medium onion, finely
chopped

½ tsp black salt

½ tsp pepper

2 tbsps rice flour

½ tsp sugar (optional)

Oil for deep frying or
shallow frying

Rinse the chickpeas under cold water, discarding any loose skins
or discoloured peas. Transfer to a large bowl and cover with
water. Put a lid or clean tea towel over the top and store in a cool
place to soak overnight.

Drain and then place the chickpeas, cumin, onion, salt and
pepper in a food processor or high speed blender and pulse until
a thick paste forms. If the mixture will not blend, add a little
warm water to loosen it. Add the rice flour and sugar, if using,
and blend again until all ingredients are well mixed.

Using floured hands, form the mixture into thick patties.

Heat the oil in a deep or shallow frying pan over a medium-high
heat until smoking. Slide the patties into the hot oil and cook
for 2-3 minutes until golden and crispy on one side. Turn with a
slotted spoon and cook the other side for a further 2 minutes or
until golden and crispy.

Remove from the pan and allow to drain on paper towel

CANNELLINI BEANS

This is another little morsel that could almost be the only thing in the pantry and still fuel those triathlon ambitions … or at least a lifestyle that includes as much outdoor play as indoor chill time. Cannellini beans are small white beans from Italy that are creamier than green peas and less mushy on the inside than kidney beans. When cooked, they become fluffy in texture and have a buttery flavour.

Cannellini beans are amazing on bread and in stews. They can be added to soup recipes to inject protein and they are lovely whipped up into a light, creamy dip, seasoned with salt and pepper.

Consider these amazing ways in which such a wee bean can have so much impact on your body.

- Each ½ cup serving contains 90 calories, which amounts to less than 5% of the daily suggested intake of 2000 for an adult. Those calories can be burned with a 10-minute swim or 9-minute jog or a night out dancing.
- Protein, the magic word: it builds muscles and helps weight loss. A ½ cup of cannellini beans contains 7g of protein, which is twice the amount in ½ cup of milk.
- Fibre has never gone out of style and there are 6g of the blood-sugar balancing nutrient in ½ cup of these scrumptious beans.
- Dietary fat is another eyebrow worrier and guess

what — cannellini beans have none of it. And yet they are so creamy, they can trick the tongue into thinking it's indulging in butter.

LEARN A RECIPE A WEEK

Just one new food a week can help form new, healthy habits. These will quickly become favourites.

CANNELLINI BEANS ON TOAST: Lightly sautee a handful of beans, drizzle in olive oil or almond butter, grind some pepper and salt and voila, a power breakfast or lunch.

CANNELLINI AND TUNA TREATS: Add a small can of beans to a small can of tuna, mix in chopped onions, lemon juice, salt and pepper and scoop into a crunchy lettuce leaf. Full of omega-3, light protein and the taste of the ocean.

WHITE BEAN SOUP: Cannellini beans are often referred to simply by their colour. They make a creamy soup blended with light amounts of onion, garlic and sprigs of rosemary to garnish and flavour.

CANNELLINI BEANS WITH SPINACH AND BACON: Start by crisping bacon in a pan, then throw in the beans and spinach. Sautee for 5 minutes — on a low heat so the beans retain the firmness — and this is a warm salad for lunch or dinner.

Four Bean Salad

A FAST AND EASY SALAD FULL OF ENERGY-BOOSTING BEANS THAT YOU CAN RUSTLE UP WITH MINIMUM FUSS

SERVES 4

2 x 400g (14oz) cans four bean mix, rinsed and drained

1 cup (60g, 2oz) tinned cannellini beans, rinsed and drained

1 cup (250g, 9oz) canned corn kernels

¼ cup (10g, ¼ oz) fresh parsley leaves, chopped

¼ cup (10g, ¼ oz) fresh coriander leaves, chopped

2 tsps fresh oregano, chopped

½ red onion, finely chopped

2 small cloves garlic, minced

2 tsps salt

1 tsp cumin

¼ tsp cayenne pepper

1 tbsps brown sugar

½ cup (125ml, 4fl oz) extra virgin olive oil

¼ cup (60ml, 2fl oz) red wine vinegar

2 tbsps fresh lemon juice

In a large bowl, add the beans, corn, fresh herbs and red onion.

In a small bowl, whisk together the rest of the ingredients thoroughly. Pour the dressing over the bean mixture and stir to combine.

Let sit for at least 1 hour to let all the flavours soak in before serving.

Mung Bean Salad

SERVES 4

2 cups (400g, 14oz) mung beans

½ cup (25g, 1oz) sundried tomatoes, roughly chopped

¼ cup (30g, 1oz) black olives, roughly chopped

2 spring onions, finely chopped

6 green pickles, chopped

¼ cup (10g, ¼ oz) parsley, chopped

2 tbsps fresh dill, chopped

4 tbsps lemon juice

3 tbsps olive oil

¼ tsp salt

Pinch of ground pepper, to taste

Wash and drain the mung beans and add to a medium-sized saucepan with 1L of water. Simmer for 40 minutes or until the beans are softened, but not squishy. Drain and rinse with cold water. Set aside to cool.

In a large bowl, combine the mung beans, sundried tomatoes, olives, spring onions, pickles, parsley and dill. In a small bowl, whisk together the lemon juice, olive oil and salt and pepper. Pour over the bean mix.

Combine all ingredients thoroughly and let it sit for an hour before serving to let the flavours mix through.

White Bean Salad

SERVES 4

1½ cups (275g, 9oz) barley

3 cups (750ml, 24fl oz) water

½ tsp salt

1 tbsp olive oil

1 clove garlic, slivered

150g (5oz) mushrooms, sliced

1 large bunch of spinach, leaves torn

2 lemons, zested

1 tbsp dill, chopped

1 x 400g (14oz) can cannellini beans, drained and rinsed

Place the barley, water and salt in a large saucepan over medium-high heat. Bring to the boil, then reduce heat to low and cover the pan. Simmer for 45 minutes, or until the liquid is absorbed. Drain and set aside.

Heat oil in a frying pan over a medium heat. Add garlic and mushrooms and cook for 5 minutes, until tender. Add spinach and a pinch of salt and cook for 1-2 minutes until spinach wilts.

Remove from heat and place into a large bowl. Stir through the barley, lemon zest, dill and white beans.

CANNELLINI
BEAN DIP

Similar to hummus, this is another little wonder dip that can be served as a nibblie and it wouldn't matter if the host never got around to dishing out the main meal. The party would continue. A staple appetiser at Italian restaurants, it is creamy and zesty and can be spread on bread the next day. It is a very simple blend of cannellini beans, garlic, salt, pepper and olive oil. A sprig of rosemary adds some bounce. And while there are ways to be inventive with this perfect puree — lemon zest or a sprinkle of chilli apparently does wonders — simplicity need not be messed with.

Red Quinoa Mango Salad

FRESH, SWEET AND CITRUS FLAVOURS COMBINE IN THIS CRACKER OF A SALAD, POWERED BY QUINOA

SERVES 4

3 cups (555g, 1¼ lb) cooked red quinoa, cooled

2 ripe mangoes, cubed

2 spring onions, sliced

¼ cup (10g, ¼ oz) fresh parsley, chopped

3 tbsps fresh coriander, chopped

Smoked paprika, to taste

CITRUS VINAIGRETTE

¼ cup (60ml, 2fl oz) fresh lemon juice

2 tbsps fresh lime juice

¼ cup (60ml, 2fl oz) olive oil

1 tsp American mustard

¼ tsp cumin

¼ tsp ground coriander

1 tsp salt

Freshly ground black pepper

In a large bowl, combine the quinoa, mango, spring onion, parsley and coriander.

To make the dressing, whisk together in a small bowl the lemon and lime juice, oil, mustard, cumin, coriander, salt and a couple of grinds of pepper.

Pour the dressing over the quinoa mixture and stir thoroughly.

Refrigerate an hour before serving and serve with a sprinkling of the paprika.

Summer Picnic Loaf

A WARMING, KID-FRIENDLY LOAF THAT YOU CAN PACK AND TAKE WITH YOU FOR A HEALTHY WEEKEND LUNCH

SERVES 6

1 punnet cherry tomatoes — mixed colours

2 tbsps olive oil

3 cups (375g, 12oz) plain flour

1 tbsp baking powder

½ tsp bicarbonate of soda

1 tsp salt

1 clove garlic, minced

1 tbsp fresh thyme, chopped

2 tbsps fresh oregano, chopped

125g (4oz) feta cheese, crumbled

2 eggs

½ cup (125ml, 4fl oz) olive oil

2 cups (500ml, 1pt) milk

500g (1lb 2oz) fresh spinach leaves, chopped

Preheat oven to 180°C (350°F, Gas Mark 4).

Grease a 22 x 13cm (10 x 5in) loaf tin.

Line a large flat baking tray with baking paper.

Cut the cherry tomatoes in half and place cut-side down on the tray. Drizzle over with the olive oil.

Bake in the oven for 30 minutes. Remove and set aside.

In a large bowl combine the flour, baking powder, bicarb, salt, garlic, herbs and feta.

In a medium bowl, stir together the eggs, oil, milk and spinach.

Add this to the flour mixture and stir to combine thoroughly. Pour this mixture into the loaf tin. Press the tomato halves into the top cut side up.

Bake in the oven for 1 hour, or until a skewer inserted in the centre comes out clean.

Crunchy Fresh Quinoa Salad

ADD GRILLED CHICKEN OR LAMB TO THIS BRIGHT SALAD FOR A FULLY-BALANCED MEAL

SERVES 2

2 Lebanese cucumbers, chopped

½ tbsp salt

3 sticks celery, chopped

1 cup (185g, 6oz) cooked white quinoa

2 spring onions, finely sliced

½ tbsps sugar

1 tbsp light soy sauce

2½ tbsps rice wine vinegar

1 tsp sesame oil

½ tbsp lemon juice

Lemon peel, for garnish

Place the cucumber in a colander and coat with the salt. Let it sit for 5 minutes to pull out some of the liquid.

Pat dry with paper towels and place in a large bowl with the celery, quinoa and spring onions.

In a small bowl, mix the sugar, soy sauce, rice wine vinegar, sesame oil and lemon and stir until the sugar has dissolved.

Pour the dressing over the quinoa mix and stir to combine.

Garnish with thin strips of lemon peel.

COLD NOODLES

The beauty of cold noodles is that they can be digested without the sleepiness that flows in after a helping of warm pasta. And yet noodles add the essential energy of a carbohydrate that a plate of vegetables might not quite muster. Also, cold noodles make excellent leftovers to take to the beach in a container after the big lunch gathering.

There are lots of varieties of noodles nowadays that either combine or do away with the standard white wheat of pasta — ingredients like egg, spinach, seaweed and, more recently, black rice are popping up in noodles and many of them are great news for people who suffer from gluten intolerance.

KNOW YOUR NOODLE

UDON NOODLES may be the athlete of the noodle world: thick and often a vibrant buttery colour. They are chewy and hearty to eat as their maker kneads the dough with heavy-duty love. Udon noodles absorb flavours well so are often served in Asian soups with meat or vegetable broths. Udon have more of a savoury flavour than regular wheat pasta and do contain gluten.

A simple cold udon salad is tossed with sesame seeds, a light oil dressing — nut oil with a dash of sesame oil is perfect — and a sprinkling of parsley and chilli flakes.

VERMICELLI can be wheat or rice based. The best and more versatile noodles both for preparing and for eating are the rice vermicelli, which are long, thin and so white they're almost clear. They need to barely hit boiling water to become super soft and so easy to slurp and chew.

They also beautifully absorb flavours. A simple lemon and oil dressing over vermicelli with a handful of leafy greens is a light, refreshing snack. They also go great with any Asian condiments. A classic Asian dressing combines rice bran oil and a splash of sesame oil, rice wine vinegar and soy sauce. Add a bunch of salad vegetables like celery, capsicum and cucumber, and sesame seeds or chilli flakes to give some extra zing. It always tastes more complicated than it is.

SOBA NOODLES are nutty in colour and flavour, grainy in texture and found in the Asian food aisle. They are made from buckwheat, though many store-bought soba noodles contain wheat also. The Japanese love the classic dish of zaru soba, which is cold buckwheat noodles with dipping sauce. Give guests chopsticks to transport mouthfuls of noodles to a little ceramic bowl of the salty, zesty dipping sauce that combines water, soy sauce and kombu (kelp). Top with shallots and a dash of that slightly crazy wasabi sauce that makes eyes water.

Soba Noodle Bowl

LUNCH IS READY IN A FLASH WITH THIS HEALTHY AND COLOURFUL ASIAN - STYLE SALAD

SERVES 2

220g (8oz) soba noodles

¼ red cabbage, finely shredded

3 spring onions, finely sliced

½ cup (25g, 1oz) carrot, grated

¼ cup (10g, ¼ oz) fresh coriander, chopped

2 tbsps sesame seeds

⅓ cup (75g, 2oz) tahini

2 tbsps rice wine vinegar

1 tbsp ginger, grated

2 tsps soy sauce

1 tsp sesame oil

½ cup (125ml, 4fl oz) water

Sea salt, to taste

In a large saucepan, boil some water and add the soba noodles. Cook according to the packet's directions until they're al dente. Drain and rinse under cold water and set aside.

In a large bowl, mix together the cabbage, spring onion, carrot, coriander and sesame seeds.

In a small bowl, stir together the tahini, rice wine vinegar, ginger, soy sauce and sesame oil. Once these are mixed, add a bit of the water at a time, whisking all the while.

Pour the tahini sauce over the noodles. Then add the noodles to the vegetables and gently stir through to combine. Add salt if needed. Serve immediately.

Summer Noodle Salad

FULL OF CRUNCH, ZEST AND SUBSTANCE, THIS SALAD WILL SET YOU UP FOR THE AFTERNOON

SERVES 2

DRESSING

1 tbsp fish sauce

1 tsp brown sugar

3 tbsps fresh lime juice

1 tbsp soy sauce

2 tbsp water

Salt and pepper to taste

SALAD

150g (5oz) rice vermicelli noodles

½ cup (80g, 3oz) fresh peas

1 carrot, julienned

2 yellow squash, julienned

2 mangoes, julienned

1 cucumber, sliced

1 tbsp fresh mint, finely chopped

2 tbsps fresh coriander, finely chopped

Salt and pepper, to taste

In a small bowl combine all the dressing ingredients and whisk together well. Set dressing aside.

Cook the rice noodles according to packet instructions, usually for about 5 minutes in boiling water. Drain and rinse with cold water, then set aside.

In a large pot of salted boiling water, boil the peas, carrot and squash in salted boiling water for 2 minutes. Then immediately rinse in cold water.

In a large bowl, combine all the salad ingredients, then pour over the dressing. Mix gently so that all ingredients are thoroughly combined. You might want to wait until you've done some mixing before adding the mango.

Cover and put in the fridge for at least half an hour before serving.

BLACK NOODLES

There are many crafty things happening in the noodle world,
such as the lightly sweet and a little bit crunchy noodles that
are literally rice turned into noodles. Black rice is more dark
purple than black and its colour is brimming with the same
antioxidant found in blueberries and all those purple fruits that
are so good. It's not processed like white rice and contains more
protein and minerals. Now, it can be wrapped around spoons
and heaped in tomato sauce as though it was fettucine, only
with a whole lot more oomph for the heart.

Black Noodle Salad

SERVES 2

80g (3oz) black rice noodles

1 tsp vegetable or canola oil

2 medium carrots, julienned

80g (3oz) snow peas, sliced

1 green chilli, sliced

1 spring onion, sliced

DRESSING

1 clove garlic, minced

3 tbsps sesame oil

1 tsp fresh ginger, grated

1½ tbsps rice wine vinegar

2 tbsps soy sauce

2 tbsps water

Cook noodles according to packet instructions. Drain, rinse and place in large bowl. In a frying pan, heat the oil. Add carrots, cook for 3 minutes until soft. Add snow peas, green chilli and spring onion and cook for a further 2 minutes. Set aside. In a small bowl, whisk together dressing ingredients. Add vegetables to the noodles, pour over dressing and toss until well combined.

Orange Beef Stir Fry

SERVES 4

2 whole oranges, 1 zested, 2 juiced

2 cloves garlic, minced

2 tsps fresh ginger, grated

2 tbsps soy sauce

1 tbsp cornflour, mixed with 1 tbsp water

2 tbsps canola or vegetable oil, divided

600g (1lb 5oz) rump steak, trimmed of fat and cut into thin strips

2 cups (80g, 3oz) small broccoli florets

1 red capsicum, sliced

200g (7oz) snow peas, ends trimmed and sliced

2 oranges, peeled and cut into segments

1 tbsp sesame seeds

3 spring onions, sliced

Place orange zest and juice in a bowl. Add garlic, ginger and soy sauce. Stir in the cornflour mix. In a large frying pan, heat 1 tbsp of oil. Brown the beef, cooking for 2 minutes. Set aside. Heat remaining oil and fry the broccoli for 4 minutes, then add capsicum and snow peas and stir fry for another 2 minutes. Reduce heat to medium and pour orange mixture into the pan, stirring. Add beef back to the pan and heat for 1 minute. Add orange segments, sesame seeds and spring onions and quickly stir through. Serve on top of Asian-style noodles.

Moroccan Lamb Tacos

A PROTEIN-PACKED FLAVOUR BOMB, THIS LITTLE TACO MAY BECOME THE HIT OF YOUR SUMMER LUNCHES

SERVES 4-6

1.3 kg (2lb, 10oz) boneless leg of lamb

¾ cup (170g, 6oz) plain Greek yoghurt

4 tbsps extra virgin olive oil

6 cloves garlic, minced

3 tbsps ground cumin

2 tsps ginger, grated

½ tsp cinnamon

2 tsps cayenne

1 tsp black pepper

½ tsp salt

2 tbsps lemon juice

3 yellow capsicums, julienned

¾ cup (25g, 1oz) fresh coriander, roughly chopped

3 limes, cut into wedges.

½ cup (140ml, 5fl oz) barbecue sauce

12 corn or flour tacos

Place the lamb on a large piece or pieces of plastic wrap in a large shallow dish.

In a small bowl, thoroughly mix together the yoghurt, oil, garlic, cumin, ginger, cinnamon, cayenne, black pepper, salt and lemon juice. Smear all over the lamb and rub it in as much as you can. Wrap the plastic around the lamb, then place it in the fridge overnight.

Preheat oven to 230°C (445°F, Gas Mark 8).

Remove the lamb from the fridge, unwrap it and place in a roasting dish and let it sit for 30 minutes. Place in the oven and roast for 40 minutes, basting every 15 minutes or so with the juices from the lamb and yoghurt mix. Remove from oven and let sit for at least 10 minutes.

TO ASSEMBLE TACOS
Thinly slice the lamb.

Heat the tacos as per the instructions on the packet.

Place a few strips of capsicum into the taco. Add some coriander and slices of lamb. Add a small amount of barbecue sauce and squeeze over some fresh lime.

Green Lentil Meatballs with Carrot Spaghetti

YOU'LL NEVER LOOK BACK WITH THIS BRIGHT VEGAN TAKE ON THE CLASSIC MEATBALLS AND SPAGHETTI DISH

SERVES 46

LENTIL MEATBALLS

½ cup (90g, 3oz) green lentils

1 bay leaf

1 cup (250ml, 8fl oz) vegetable stock

2 tbsp ground flaxseed

225g (8oz) button mushroom

1 cup (90g, 3oz) rolled oats

½ cup (85g, 3oz) cannellini beans

½ cup (10g, ¼ oz) parsley

2 tsps mixed herbs

1 tbsp olive oil

1 small onion, finely chopped

½ tsp salt

Pepper, to taste

3 cloves garlic, minced

¼ cup (60ml, 2fl oz) red wine vinegar

1 tbsp soy sauce

CARROT SPAGHETTI

8 carrots

Squeeze of lemon

Sea salt and pepper, to taste

Preheat oven to 200°C (400°F, Gas Mark 6) and line a baking tray with baking paper.

Place the lentils, bay leaf and vegetable stock in a medium saucepan, and bring to the boil. Reduce heat to a simmer and cook for 10 minutes or until almost all the liquid is absorbed. Remove bay leaf and set aside to cool for a few minutes.

In a small bowl, combine flaxseed and ¼ cup of warm water. Stir and set aside until a gel forms.

Combine the mushrooms, oats, beans, parsley and mixed herbs in a food processor and process until roughly chopped. Add the lentils and flax gel and gently pulse until mixture is combined and well chopped.

In a medium saucepan over medium-high heat, combine olive oil, onions, salt and pepper. Cook for 6-8 minutes until translucent and beginning to caramelise. Add garlic and cook for another 1-2 minutes. Add vinegar and soy sauce and cook until most of the liquid has evaporated.

In a large bowl, combine lentil mixture and onions. When cool enough to handle, roll mixture into balls and place them on the prepared baking tray. Continue until there is no mixture remaining.

Transfer to the oven to bake for 25-30 minutes or until meatballs are golden brown and cooked through.

To make the spaghetti, cut carrots into thin strips using a spiraliser if you have one. If not, a mandolin, box grater or even a knife will do. Saute carrots in a pan over a medium heat with a little olive oil. Season with lemon, sea salt and black pepper.

Divide carrots between serving plates and serve with meatballs.

Falafel Lunch Box

THESE LITTLE NUTRIENT BALLS TASTE FANTASTIC HOT FROM THE PAN OR TAKE THEM WITH YOU FOR A COLD LUNCH

SERVES 4

FALAFEL

½ red onion, roughly chopped

2 cloves garlic, minced

1 green chilli, seeds removed

2 cups (60g, 2oz) parsley, roughly chopped

1 cup (40g, 1oz) coriander, roughly chopped

2 x 400g (14oz) cans chickpeas, rinsed and drained

1 tbsp cumin

Pinch of paprika

1 tsp salt

1 tbsp lemon juice

¼ cup (30g, 1oz) plain flour

½ tsp baking powder

Oil for frying

SALAD

1 cup (190g, 7oz) couscous

2 tbsps olive oil

2 spring onions, sliced

¼ tsp turmeric

1 small Lebanese cucumber, sliced

1 x 250g (9oz) block of Greek feta, cubed

¼ cup (15g, ½ oz) semi-sundried tomatoes, chopped

½ head of red cabbage, finely shredded

¼ cup (10g, ¼oz) coriander, roughly chopped

Lime wedges to garnish

YOGHURT DIPPING SAUCE

1 cup (225g, 8oz) Greek yoghurt

1 clove garlic, minced

Salt and pepper to taste

Pinch of paprika

Cook the couscous according to the instructions on the packet.

Toss the warm cooked couscous with the olive oil, spring onions and tumeric. Set aside and let cool.

To make the falafel, place the red onion, garlic, chilli, parsley, coriander, chickpeas, cumin, paprika and salt in a food processor and pulse several times until everything is finely chopped. The more you blend it, the more like a paste the mix will become. Try not to let it turn into too much of paste. Scrape down the sides of the blender as you go to ensure everything is finely chopped.

Transfer the falafel mix to a large bowl. Mix through the lemon juice, flour and baking powder. Use a dessertspoon to measure out small amounts of the mixture and shape into small balls. Flatten each one slightly.

In a medium deep saucepan, heat some oil to medium-high. You need enough oil to generously cover at least four falafel at a time as you fry them. Fry the falafel in batches until they're a golden to dark brown and crispy on the outside. Place them on paper towels to absorb excess oil.

While the falafel are cooling, in a medium bowl, mix together the yoghurt and garlic and add salt and pepper to taste. Place into small dip bowl and sprinkle over the paprika.

Serve falafel over the couscous with the cucumber, feta, sundried tomatoes and cabbage on the side. Sprinkle over some coriander as well as a squeeze of lime.

Thai Beef Salad

THIS EASY, TASTY, PROTEIN-PACKED DISH IS A CLASSIC THAT SHOULD BE ON EVERY COOK'S LIST OF GO-TO MEALS

SERVES 4

MARINADE

2 cloves garlic, chopped

2 tbsps coriander, chopped

2 tbsps water

2 tbsps fish sauce

1 tbsp palm sugar (or brown sugar)

3 tbsps lime juice

BEEF SALAD

600g (1lb 5oz) beef fillet

Salt and pepper, to season

½ red onion, sliced

1 cucumber, julienned

2 carrots, julienned

1 bunch spinach, leaves picked

Handful of watercress

Handful of beansprouts

Sesame seeds

Make the marinade: combine all the ingredients in a small bowl and whisk together. Set aside.

Trim the meat of fat and season with salt and pepper on both sides.

Place the beef on a hot grill and cook for 3-4 minutes each side according to how rare you'd like the meat. Remove from heat and place the meat in a shallow dish with sides to it. Pour the marinade over the meat. Allow to rest, covered in foil, for 10 minutes. Slice the meat.

Arrange the salad vegetables on serving plate. Top with the sliced, rested beef and any remaining juices from the dish. Garnish with sesame seeds then serve.

POLENTA

Polenta is a creamy dish that in its most basic form has the consistency of porridge and a mildly cheesy taste with a hint of honey sweetness. It is made from cornmeal, which is corn that is ground into different consistencies. Basic polenta is made from medium to fine cornmeal and boiled with water or milk and salt to make a warming porridge. This can be seasoned with salt and pepper and eaten on its own or baked and fried into pizza or pie bases as well as sweet treats.

Adding polenta to the diet is a good way to eat less rice, pasta and potato, all of which are delicious yet not great for the waistline and also have that pesky sleep-inducing effect. The best role that polenta plays in an active diet: it is a perfect substitute for mashed potato — polenta that's boiled up with milk comes out creamy and fluffy. Polenta has more protein than the other carbohydrates, which converts into energy. It is also an excellent source of iron, magnesium, phosphorous, zinc and vitamin B6.

Polenta is usually found in the pasta and flour aisles of supermarkets. There are quite a few different types of polenta sold and it's tempting to go for the instant kind, but this tends to contain added ingredients and preservatives, which take away some of the health benefits of the unprocessed polenta. The best option is to buy the polenta grain, which is usually readily available, and cook it from scratch, which takes about 40 minutes.

Pre-cooked polenta is also a fun option — it's sold in tubes, usually in a supermarket's refrigerated section. Grab one, chop it into smooth shapes — it cuts like butter — and stick it in a frying pan for a savoury snack.

Polenta will last for six months if kept in an airtight container in either a cool cupboard or in the fridge. So, there is always a cheap and energizing snack waiting to go.

A FEW SPECIAL (SIMPLE) POLENTA IDEAS

POLENTA WITH PARMESAN: Add parmesan and butter to the basic boil of polenta and water. It's cheesy and delicious and packs an extra punch of protein.

BREAKFAST POLENTA: Add a fried egg and gently sautéed spinach to the above and there's a hearty brunch. Roasted tomatoes will add a vitamin C–packed saucy touch.

HOT POLENTA CHIPS: These can be more delicious than takeaway hot chips … and they are baked, not fried. Buy the pre-cooked polenta in a tube. Cut into finger-length rectangles, season with pepper and maybe some basil flakes, moisten with olive oil and bake for 40 minutes.

Polenta Quiche Florentine

A NUTRITIOUS OPTION FOR AN EASY WORKDAY LUNCH THAT CAN BE MADE BEFOREHAND AND WARMED UP IN A MINUTE

SERVES 8

CRUST

1½ cups (375ml, 13fl oz) vegetable stock

½ tsp salt

1¼ cups (200g, 7oz) polenta

1 egg, lightly beaten

½ cup (60g, 2oz) Parmesan cheese, grated

1¼ cups (310ml, 10fl oz) water

FILLING

1½ tbsps olive oil

2 red onions, halved and thinly sliced

1½ cups (50g, 2oz) baby spinach

6 large basil leaves, thinly shredded

5 large eggs

½ cup (125ml, 4fl oz) cream

½ cup (125ml, 4fl oz) milk

¼ tsp salt

Pinch of nutmeg

1 cup (120g, 4oz) mozzarella, grated

Preheat the oven to 190°C (375°F, Gas Mark 5).

To make the crust, heat the stock in a medium saucepan until boiling. Add the salt and slowly pour the polenta into the water in a thin stream, stirring vigorously the whole time. Reduce the heat and cook for 10 minutes, stirring almost constantly to prevent the polenta from sticking to the bottom of the saucepan.

Stir the egg and Parmesan through the polenta thoroughly.

Lightly grease a 25cm (10in) pie dish with olive oil. Press the polenta mix into the dish. If it begins to get sticky, have a glass of cold water on hand. Dip your fingers or spoon into the water and that will prevent it from sticking.

FILLING

In a medium saucepan heat the olive oil over a medium heat. Add the red onion and cook for 5 minutes until slightly softened. Add the spinach and basil, a handful at a time, and cook until just wilted. Remove from the heat and set aside.

In a large bowl, beat the eggs and add the cream, milk, salt and nutmeg. Beat them as briskly as you can. You want the mixture to be light and fluffy. Gently stir through the mozzarella and onion mixture.

Pour the mixture into the pie dish. Fill as much as you can without letting any liquid spill over the edges.

Bake for 45 minutes, until the quiche is browned and set in the middle.

Vegan Polenta Pizza

A GLUTEN-FREE PIZZA OPTION THAT WILL SURPRISE YOU WITH HOW SIMPLE IT IS TO MAKE AND HOW GOOD IT TASTES

SERVES 6

BASE

2 cups (500ml, 1pt) vegetable stock

½ tsp salt

½ tsp dried basil

1 tbsp olive oil

¾ cup (120g, 4oz) polenta

TOPPING

4 tbsps olive oil

2 cups (150g, 5oz) small button mushrooms, sliced

¾ cup (180g, 6oz) tomato puree

1½ cups (50g, 2oz) baby spinach leaves

1 punnet cherry tomatoes, halved

1 red onion, sliced

To make the base, heat the stock in a medium saucepan until boiling. Add the salt, basil and olive oil and then slowly pour the polenta into the water in a thin stream, stirring vigorously the whole time. Reduce the heat and cook for 10 minutes, stirring almost constantly to prevent the polenta from sticking to the bottom of the saucepan.

Line a large flat baking tray with baking paper and lightly brush it with olive oil. Press the polenta mix onto the paper in a thin layer into your desired pizza shape. If it begins to get sticky, have a glass of cold water on hand. Dip your fingers or a spoon into the water and that will prevent it from sticking.

Place the tray in the fridge for 30 minutes until cool.

TOPPING

Preheat oven to 220°C (430°F, Gas Mark 7).

Heat 2 tablespoons of the oil in a large frying pan on medium heat. Add the mushrooms and lightly cook for 5 minutes. Don't overcook them as they'll cook further in the oven. Remove the mushrooms from the heat and set aside.

Remove your pizza base from the fridge and brush over the remaining olive oil. Bake in the oven for 15 minutes.

Remove from oven and spread the tomato puree over the base. Lay the spinach leaves over the sauce, then add the mushrooms, tomatoes, and onion.

Bake for in the oven for 15 minutes. The edges of the pizza base should be just beginning to brown. Remove and let it sit for at least 10 minutes before serving, to allow the base to firm up.

Rice and Ricotta Pie

A SAVOURY TAKE ON A CLASSIC MEDITTERANEAN FAVOURITE THAT'S HEARTY AND GREAT FOR LUNCHBOXES AND PICNICS

SERVES 8

BASE

1 tsp olive oil

2 cups (450g, 1lb) cooked brown rice

3 tbsps Parmesan cheese, grated

PIE

2 tbsps olive oil

1 large onion, finely chopped

3 eggs, lightly beaten

500g (1lb 2oz) fresh ricotta cheese

½ cup (60g, 2oz) tasty cheese, grated

1 cup (30g, 1oz) fresh spinach, finely chopped

½ tsp pepper

¼ tsp salt

Pinch of nutmeg

Preheat oven to 190°C (375°F, Gas Mark 5).

BASE

Lightly grease a 25cm (10inch) pie dish with olive oil. In a medium bowl, stir through the rice and Parmesan. Press the mix into the pie dish and about 2cm (1in) up along the sides. If the mixture becomes too sticky, have some water ready. Dip your fingers in and that should prevent it from sticking.

FILLING

In a large bowl, thoroughly mix all the filling ingredients. Place onto the rice base and cook for 45 minutes or until the edges are browned and the filling is set in the middle.

Mushrooms on Polenta Toast

SERVES 4

1½ cups (240g, 8oz) polenta

2 tbsps olive oil

700g (1½ lb) button mushrooms, halved

½ cup (20g, ¾ oz) fresh basil, shredded

1 tbsp fresh parsley, finely chopped

½ tsp black pepper

¼ tsp salt

Preheat oven to 200°C (400°F, Gas Mark 6). Cook the polenta on the stovetop according to the instructions on packet. Butter a slice tin. Pour the polenta into this and smooth the surface. Bake in the oven for 15 minutes, until firm and lightly browned. Set aside to cool.

In a large frying pan, heat the oil. Add the mushrooms and cook for 6 minutes — use more oil as needed. Add the basil, parsley, pepper and salt and heat through for 2 minutes.

Cut the polenta into squares, and serve with the cooked mushroom mix on top.

Polenta Syrup Cake

SERVES 6

200g (7oz) butter at room temperature

¾ cup (165g, 6oz) caster sugar

3 large eggs at room temperature

2 small oranges, zested and juiced

2 cups (250g, 8oz) almond flour

¾ cup (120g, 4oz) polenta

1 tsp baking powder

½ cup (180g, 6oz) maple syrup

Preheat oven to 180°C (350°F, Gas Mark 4). Grease a round springform cake tin.

Using a mixer, beat together butter and sugar until light and fluffy. Add eggs, one at a time, ensuring each one is incorporated. Mix through the orange zest, then stir in the almond flour, polenta and baking powder. Pour cake mix into tin and bake for 1 hour, until a skewer comes out clean. Sit cake on a wire rack in tin to cool.

In a small saucepan, gently heat the maple syrup and orange juice until boiling. Prick the cake all over with a skewer and pour the hot syrup evenly over the cake. Remove the cake from the tin and serve.

MARMALADE

There's something about a pot of marmalade that says 'fresh' and adds zing, which is not just a feeling — good marmalade can give a similar immune-system boost and energy rush as a fresh juice shot. The classic marmalade is orange and there are hundreds of versions of it out there. The most important thing if you are making it at home is to use whole, fresh oranges for maximum flavour and vitamin C. And it can be spread on toast without butter without flinching.

Power
Smoothies

GREEN VEGGIES

'Eat your greens' is a favourite expression at many family dinner tables. It can take a bit of a shift in mindset to steam up a bowl of broccoli for afternoon tea or maybe a plate of bok choy splashed with soy sauce. But adding sprinkles of cheese or bacon to most vegetables makes them tastier than chips, plus they're full of protein.

Later, at dinner time, aim to fill a quarter of the plate with greens, and another quarter with veggies of different colours like red, yellow and orange. Each colour corresponds with a type of nutrients and the closer to a rainbow, the closer to a well-rounded diet.

THREE OF THE BEST

SPINACH. Popeye made its turbo strength famous: a tin of spinach made his arms bulge. Half a cup of spinach, lightly boiled and drained, injects 3.2g of iron, which is 20% of the daily iron requirement. Iron is great for arm muscles and crucial for energy — a lack of iron is a common cause of fatigue.

WHEN SHOPPING: remember that silverbeet, chard, kale and spinach are all big-leaf green vegetables — silverbeet has a thick white stem running up its middle, chard often has bright red stems and kale is often crinkled around the edges. For all of these veggies the leaves should be vibrant and fresh, not wilted or yellow. Do the 'snap' test to check the stems are firm and fresh. If the stems make a healthy crunch when snapped, all is well and ready for an iron feast.

BROCCOLI. It is everyone's most or least favourite vegetable … and it is a powerhouse of nutrients, so it seems a good idea to train the taste buds to love it. Broccoli's best traits are oodles of vitamin C and vitamin A, potassium and folate.

WHEN SHOPPING: look for buds that are bright and vibrant green and also compact—if the buds are separating, the broccoli may be old and susceptible to mould. Microwaving broccoli retains more nutrients than boiling. Steaming avoids potential risks that some say come with using the microwave.

BOK CHOY. Green leaves attach to a crunchy stem that can be white or green. It has a slightly pungent flavour — like somebody took a pepper grinder to a plate of cabbage. Eating two bok choy 'trees' is more nutritious than taking a multivitamin in the morning, as it includes the energy boosts of protein and fibre. A cup of shredded raw bok choy contains about half of the daily requirement for vitamin A, C, B6 and vitamin KPlus, which helps the blood stream stay healthy after bruising and injuries.

WHEN SHOPPING: the more vibrant the green, the fresher the veg. Gently squeeze the stems to feel the crunch — if rubbery, they might be old. Avoid any with brown or black spots, which indicates decay.

The Green Day Smoothie

GET YOUR DAY OFF TO A GREAT START WITH THIS GLASS OF GREEN GOODNESS — POWERED BY CHIA SEEDS

SERVES 2

1 avocado, peeled and pitted

1 banana (frozen)

1 tbsp chia seeds

Handful of rocket, washed (optional)

1 small bunch spinach, washed

½ lime, peeled

¼ cucumber, peeled and chopeed

1 cup (250ml, 8fl oz) water

Extra chia seeds, to garnish

Add all the ingredients to a blender and process until smooth enough to drink.

Pour into glasses, garnish with extra chia seeds and serve immediately.

NOTE: If you don't have rocket, don't worry, it's fine without. Rocket is peppery and gives a bit of extra zing if that's to your liking.

Cashew Nut Milk

THIS MILK IS A GREAT BASE FOR SMOOTHIES — ESPECIALLY IF YOU ARE CUTTING OUT DAIRY — AND SO EASY

SERVES 2

1 cup (125g, 4oz) raw cashews

Water, for soaking

3 cups (750ml, 24fl oz) water

Pinch of salt

TO SWEETEN

1 tsp vanilla extract

4 pitted dates

2 tbsps maple syrup

Place the nuts in a bowl or glass jar and cover with enough water to sit about 2cm (1in) above the nuts. Place a plate or clean tea towel over the top and set aside to soak at room temperature for 2 hours. Soaking will activate the cashew nuts.

Drain nuts and rinse well under cool water. Discard the soaking liquid.

Place the cashews, 3 cups of water and salt in a blender and process at the highest possible speed for 1-2 minutes, until smooth and creamy.

NOTES: Store the milk in a sealed container in the fridge for 2 to 3 days.

To make sweet milk add the vanilla, dates and maple syrup at the time of blending.

Raspberry Herb Crush

A FRESH, FRUITY AND REFRESHING DRINK THAT WILL GET YOU GOING AND COOL YOU DOWN

SERVES 2

225g (8oz, ½ lb) raspberries, hulled and frozen

½ cup (115g, 4oz) yoghurt

1 cup (250ml, 8fl oz) coconut water

1 tbsp honey

½ cup (75g, 3oz) ice cubes

Large handful of parsley leaves

Handful of mint leaves (retain a couple for garnish)

Add all the ingredients except garnish to your blender and blend until smooth enough to drink.

Add more coconut water if required to reach desired consistency.

Pour into glasses, garnish with mint and serve immediately.

NOTE: For the dairy-free, this smoothie will work perfectly fine without the yoghurt. Add a little more ice for a thicker consistency.

Chocolate Nut Sunday

FOR BREAKFAST, DESSERT OR AFTERNOON TEA, THIS SMOOTHIE MAKES FOR A CREAMY AND DELICIOUS TREAT

SERVES 4

2 avocados

½ cup (60g, 2oz) whole almonds

3 frozen bananas, cut into chunks

4 cups (1L, 2pt) almond milk

2 tsps maple syrup

3 tbsps cacao powder

4 tsps almonds, sliced, to garnish

Extra cacao powder, to garnish

Add all the ingredients except garnish to your blender and blend until smooth enough to drink.

Pour into glasses, garnish with sliced almonds and cacao powder and serve immediately.

Busy Bee Smoothie

SERVES 2-3

1 banana

2 small beetroots, peeled

½ cup (60g, 2oz) raspberries

½ cup (115g, 4oz) plain Greek yoghurt

½ cup (125ml, 4fl oz) milk

1 tbsp bee pollen

2 tsps lime juice

1 cup (150g, 5oz) ice cubes

1 tsp bee pollen and coconut flakes, to garnish

Add all the ingredients except garnish to the blender and process until smooth enough to drink.

Add more milk if required to reach desired consistency.

Pour into glasses, garnish with bee pollen and coconut flakes and serve immediately.

Detoxify Smoothie

SERVES 2

1 pear, cored and quartered

1 stalk celery

1 cup (250ml, 8fl oz) almond milk

½ bunch spinach, washed

1 tsp flaxseed

1 tbsp chia seeds

1 cup (150g, 5oz) ice cubes

Chia and flaxseeds, to garnish

Add all the ingredients except garnish to the blender and process until smooth enough to drink.

Add more milk if required to reach desired consistency.

Pour into a glass, garnish with seeds and serve immediately.

FLAXSEED

Flaxseeds, also known as linseeds, are small, brown, tan or golden-colored seeds that are the richest sources of a plant-based omega-3 fatty acids, called alpha-linolenic acid (ALA) in the world. This ALA does need to be converted by the body to be effective, however, and that's not always easy. Nonetheless flaxseeds are fully of healthy fats and fibre, and have a lovely nutty flavour, so by adding them to your smoothie you will feel full and satisfied – minus the calories!

GOJI BERRIES

These pea-sized berries are originally from China and have been declared a 'superfood', which just means that they have a lot of vitamins and minerals. When dried, they are red like a raspberry, scrunched like raisins and taste like a sour cherry.

Part of their appeal to nutritionists and chefs is their history — they have long been used in ancient Chinese medicine to help in the healing of all sorts of ailments including diabetes, hypertension, arthritis and fevers. As with many Chinese remedies, there is no scientific proof to back up these claims, but there are plenty of other health benefits that are proven.

What is known is that goji berries are full of fibre, which is what the body needs to get rid of toxins and excess nutrients and water that can cause fatigue. It's also known that goji berries are pumping with micronutrients like vitamin A, vitamin C and iron, and contain all of the eight essential amino acids humans need to stay refreshed and repaired, especially during and after exercise.

TIPS FOR THE SHOPPING AISLE

Goji berries are not the cheapest fruit to buy, as can happen with foods that become trendy. Also, the bushes can take up to four years to flower and the berries require some intense labour for picking and preparing.

They are usually sold in dried form, so come chewy and ready to eat or cook with. Check the package label to make sure there are no added sugars or preservatives like sulfur dioxide, which is sometimes added to dried fruits to help preserve colour. The berries don't need the preservative and will last for a year if stored in a cool, dry place or the fridge.

Goji berry powder is also popular and sold in most health-food stores or the health-food aisle of supermarkets. They can also be bought online when supplies are low.

HOW TO EAT AND COOK WITH GOJI BERRIES

Goji berries can be eaten straight from the packet or soaked in hot water to soften the texture and mellow out the sour taste. And then, get creative. They are a great addition to scroggin for snacks on a day-long bike ride. Throw them into yoghurt with some honey and nutmeg and blend them into a smoothie. Garnish cereals and salads for zesty mouthfuls.

Or steam the scrunchy little things with a plate of green vegetables — the herby, tart flavour sweetens with the heat. Or throw a handful into a rice salad along with some walnuts and a mild dressing of olive oil and chives.

Peach Cream Smoothie

A DREAMY PEACHY DRINK THAT'S BOTH FILLING AND REFRESHING AND COULD BE BREAKFAST ON THE RUN

SERVES 2

1½ cups (375ml, 13fl oz) soy milk (or nut milk of choice)

3 peaches, pitted

1 banana (frozen)

½ cup (115g, 4oz) pumpkin puree (fresh or frozen)

½ (40g, 1½ oz) oats

1 tbsp honey

½ tsp vanilla extract

1 cup (150g, 5oz) ice cubes

Oats and goji berries, to garnish

Add all the ingredients except garnish to your blender and blend until smooth enough to drink.

Pour into glasses. Garnish with oats and goji berries, and serve immediately.

Goji Go Go Smoothie

THIS HEALTHY POWER SMOOTHIE HAS THE DING-A-LING ZING TO GET YOU UP AND RUNNING EVERY DAY

SERVES 1

2 tbsps goji berries

½ cup (115g, 4oz) plain yoghurt

1 cup (250ml, 8fl oz) coconut water

½ cup (100g, 4oz) lychees (fresh or frozen)

Juice of half a lime

1 cup (150g, 5oz) ice cubes

Add all the ingredients to the blender and process until smooth enough to drink.

Pour into glasses and serve immediately.

Turmeric Coconut Smoothie

SERVES 2

1½ cups (300g, 11oz) pineapple (frozen)

1 banana (frozen)

1 tbsp fresh turmeric, grated (or 1 tsp ground turmeric)

1 tbsp chia seeds

1 tbsp shredded coconut

1 tsp rice malt syrup (or honey)

2 cups (500ml, 1pt) coconut water

Add all the ingredients to the blender and process until smooth enough to drink.

Pour into bottles or glasses and serve immediately.

Nut Spice Smoothie

SERVES 2

1 cup (250ml, 8fl oz) coconut water

4 apples, stewed

½ cup (60g, 2oz) raw cashew nuts

½ tsp vanilla extract

½ tsp ground cinnamon

½ tsp ground nutmeg

2 tbsps maple syrup

1 cup (150g, 5oz) ice cubes

Place the cashews in a bowl and cover with water. Soak for 4 hours. Drain.

Add all the ingredients to the blender and process until smooth enough to drink.

Pour into glasses and sprinkle with cinnamon or add a cinnamon stick to serve.

TURMERIC

Tumeric is ancient spice currently making a big comeback. The roots, like those of ginger, are full of goodness and these are the part that's used in medicine and food. Curcumin, the active ingredient, has antioxindant properties and has been used in both Ayurvedic and Chinese medicine as an anti-inflammatory, to treat digestive and liver problems, skin diseases and wounds. A word of warning: be careful when you are peeling fresh turmeric as it will stain everything from your fingers to your kitchen bench. If this happens, try rubbing a little bicarbonate of soda and water together to form a paste and use this to scrub away at those turmeric stains.

Tropical Sunrise Smoothie

A GREAT WAY TO KICK START YOUR DAY — WITH THE TASTE OF SUNSHINE AND SPICE. ALOHA!

SERVES 2

1 mango, peeled and pitted

1 cup (200g, 7oz) pineapple (fresh or frozen)

¾ cup (185ml, 6fl oz) coconut water

1 lime, juiced

¼ cup (50g, 2oz) plain yoghurt

2 tsp rice malt syrup

½ tsp ground turmeric

¼ tsp ground cardamom

Add all the ingredients to the blender and process until smooth enough to drink.

Pour into glasses and serve immediately.

Peanut Butter Chocolate Smoothie

A GREAT BREAKFAST IDEA FOR THE KIDS — NO-ONE WILL BE ABLE TO RESIST DRINKING THIS CHOCOLATE NUT CREATION

SERVES 2

2 bananas (fresh or frozen)

1 cup (250ml, 8fl oz) milk

1 cup (225g, 8oz) plain Greek yoghurt

½ cup (40g, 1½ oz) rolled oats

1 tbsp cocoa

¼ cup (90g, 3oz) natural peanut butter

½ tsp vanilla extract

1 cup (150g, 5oz) ice cubes

Extra cocoa and chopped peanuts, to garnish

Add all the ingredients except garnish to the blender and process until smooth enough to drink.

Add more milk if required to reach desired consistency.

Pour into glasses, garnish with cocoa and nuts and serve immediately.

NOTE: The peanut-sensitive can swap almond butter for peanuts in this recipe.

Morning Coffee Smoothie

A PERFECT WAY TO TAKE YOUR COFFEE ON A HOT SUMMER'S DAY — STAY COOL AND REFUEL

SERVES 1

1 tsp instant coffee, or ½ cup (125ml, 4fl oz) brewed coffee, chilled

1 tsp cocoa powder

1 tsp coconut sugar (or honey)

1 cup (250ml, 8fl oz) coconut milk

¼ tsp cinnamon (plus more to garnish)

1 cup (150g, 5oz) ice cubes

1 tsp maca powder (optional)

Add all the ingredients to the blender and process until smooth enough to drink. Add more milk if required to reach desired consistency.

Pour into a tall glass, garnish with cinnamon and serve immediately.

NOTE: This drink can also be made with cow's milk for a closer match to a regular coffee. For a creamy top, add frothed milk or whipped cream.

MATCHA

There has been a new ingredient popping up on cafe menus of late: matcha powder is being frothed into minty green lattes at trendy coffee shops or sprinkled over breakfast and lunch plates.

The appeal of matcha is its interesting balance of effects on energy levels: it has a calming effect and also increases energy and endurance. It's not caffeine that makes the magic happen — the process of grinding green tea leaves into matcha brings out different nutrients from what is contained in black tea. The leaves have not been oxidized like the leaves of black tea and contain many antioxidants, including the potent catechin — pronounced 'cat-e-kin', which boosts metabolism. Matcha also contains an amino acid called L-theanine that induces relaxation without the drowsiness or the edginess that coffee often causes. It's kind of like swinging in a hammock for hours without falling asleep.

TRY A NEW HABIT

Decide to drink a matcha latte once or twice a week, instead of a triple-shot long black. The flavour is nutty and lightly sweet and the fineness of the powder produces a creamy yet light froth. And there's something about a cup of lime green milk in the morning. The physical boost might feel different from the coffee at first but living without 'the jitters' of coffee might become addictive.

MAKE YOUR OWN LATTE

A matcha latte doesn't require a special machine or technique, just the right ingredients and a few moments for preparing.

½ tsp matcha green tea powder — available in the health-food aisles of supermarkets
¼ cup very hot water (but not boiling)
1 cup milk (coconut, almond or cow's milk), heated to a hot (but not boiling) temperature
¼ tsp cinnamon
Pinch of nutmeg
¼ tsp honey or maple syrup

1. Scoop matcha powder into a small wide bowl, then slowly pour in the hot water using a teaspoon to stir. Add the honey and keep stirring.
2. Pour the heated milk into a teacup or mug, then add the matcha-honey mixture. Stir well.
3. Sprinkle with nutmeg and cinnamon and serve immediately. Simple!

FUN DINNER PARTY TIP

In Japan, matcha tea is given the way a bottle of wine or a bouquet of flowers is in Australia. It is revered as a special and thoughtful gift.

Matcha Mint Smoothie

IS GREEN. IS GOOD. IS MATCHA. IS EVEN BETTER. ENJOY THIS AWESOME GLASS OF GOODNESS TO START YOUR DAY

SERVES 2

1 banana (frozen)

2-3 stems kale, washed and tough stalks removed

Handul of mint leaves

1 kiwi fruit, peeled and chopped

1 tbsp matcha green tea powder

1 cup (250ml, 8fl oz) coconut water

1 tbsp flaxseed

1-2 tbsps maple syrup

Pinch of sea salt

½ cup (75g, 3oz) ice cubes

Add all the ingredients to the blender and process until smooth enough to drink.

Pour into glasses and serve immediately.

NOTE: If the taste of kale is too strong for you, try substituting spinach, which is much milder in flavour.

Matcha Chia Smoothie Bowl

AN EASY, DELICIOUS AND NUTRITIOUS BREAKFAST OPTION THAT WILL HAVE YOU FIRING ON ALL CYLINDERS

SERVES 1

4 tbsps chia seeds

1 tsp vanilla extract

1½ cups (375ml, 13fl oz) coconut milk

1 kiwi fruit, peeled and quartered

1 banana (frozen)

½ cup (125ml, 4fl oz) coconut water

1 tbsp matcha green tea

TO SERVE

Handful of fresh or frozen raspberries

Spoonful of coconut yoghurt

Place the chia seeds in a medium-sized bowl. Pour over the vanilla and coconut milk and stir. Set aside to soak for 20 minutes until a gel forms.

Place the kiwi fruit, banana, coconut water and matcha green tea in the blender and process until smooth.

Pour the mixture over the chia seed gel and gently stir to combine.

Transfer to a serving bowl, then top with raspberries and yoghurt to serve.

KIWI FRUIT

If you're feeling blue, try a bit of green. The colourful little kiwi fruit is reported to help with regulating mood and sleep. The reason why is all to do with the high levels of serotonin the fruit contains. Serotonin is critical in sleep, helping you to nod off, and stay asleep too, by regulating movement through the stages of sleep and interacting with the hormone melatonin, known for regulating the body's circadian rhythm. It also helps to stimulate wakefulness in the morning, helping you nail that whole asleep-at-night awake-in-the-morning thing. Pretty cool for a little green fruit.

Kiwi Gold Smoothie

SERVES 2

2 gold kiwi fruits, peeled and sliced

¼ cantaloupe, peeled and cubed

1 whole mango, peeled, pitted and cubed

1 cup (150g, 5oz) ice cubes

Sprig of mint, to garnish

Add all the ingredients except garnish to the blender and process until smooth enough to drink.

Pour into glasses, garnish with mint leaves and melon slices and serve immediately.

Green Cleanse Smoothie

SERVES 2

1 banana (frozen)

Handful of almonds

1 tsp spirulina (optional)

3 celery sticks

1 green apple, cored

1 cup (250ml, 8fl oz) coconut water

½ bunch spinach, washed

½ lemon, peeled

1 cup (150g, 5oz) ice cubes

Add all the ingredients to the blender and process until smooth enough to drink.

Pour into glasses and serve immediately.

Kiwi and Berry Smoothie

NO NEED TO DECIDE BETWEEN CREAMY BERRIES AND GREEN GOODNESS — HAVE BOTH IN THIS CHEEKY LAYERED SMOOTHIE

SERVES 1

BOTTOM LAYER

1 kiwi fruit, peeled and chopped

1 kiwi fruit, peeled and sliced

Handful of spinach leaves

Juice of 1 lime

½ cup (75g, 3oz) ice cubes

TOP LAYER

½ cup (100g, 4oz) raspberries (frozen)

½ cup (100g, 4oz) blueberries (frozen)

½ cup (125g, 4oz) yoghurt

Splash of coconut water

1 tbsp honey

Add the ingredients for the bottom layer, except for the kiwi slices, to the blender and process until smooth.

Pour this mixture into the serving glass. Place whole kiwi fruit slices down the sides of the glass and transfer to the freezer for 10 minutes while preparing top layer.

Using a clean blender, add the ingredients for the top layer to the blender and process until smooth. Add coconut water to achieve desired consistency.

Remove smoothie from the freezer. Pour berry mixture on top of the kiwi mixture and serve immediately.

Super Berry Smoothie

A LOW-FAT, HIGH-ENERGY, NUTRIENT-BURSTING SMOOTHIE THAT'S PACKED FULL OF ANTIOXIDANT BERRIES

SERVES 2

1 cup (200g, 7oz) blackberries (frozen or fresh)

½ cup (50g, 2oz) blueberries (frozen or fresh)

1 tbsp chia seeds

1 cup (250ml, 8fl oz) coconut water

½ tsp vanilla extract

½ bunch mint leaves, washed

1 cup (150g, 5oz) ice cubes

Add all the ingredients to your blender and blend until smooth enough to drink.

Pour into glasses, garnish with a few extra berries and serve immediately.

Nutritious Dinners

BROWN RICE

Brown rice used to be a hippy food — staple fare at music festivals and protests in the 1960s. Now, it's embraced by foodies, athletes and energetic people.

Becoming a lover of brown rice can take a bit of a shift — white rice is a little softer, sweeter and slightly easier to cook up for a quick snack. But brown rice has a nutty, savoury flavour, which white rice doesn't. And it still has the bran layers of the original plant, which are stripped to make white rice and some nutrients and energy-giving qualities are lost in that process. Bran means fibre — the great cleansing substance.

HOW TO COOK THE PERFECT BROWN RICE

Brown rice is slightly trickier than white rice to cook because of its fibrous outer hull, which the water needs to soften. Overcooking brown rice can lead to a mound of mush — which is ok; try adding maple syrup, walnuts and milk to turn it into breakfast.

For dinner-time brown rice, most package labels suggest boiling twice as much water as rice, then simmering for 40 minutes, until all the liquid is absorbed. There's a craftier method that only takes a few extra minutes.

- Rinse the rice in cool water.
- Boil a cup of rice in four cups of water for 30 minutes then drain the rice, as though it's pasta.
- Add a third of a cup of boiling water to the pan — just enough to coat the saucepan again.
- Scoop the rice into a colander that sits comfortably in the saucepan. Let the steam rise through the rice to preserve yet tenderise its fibre coating.
- Fluff the rice with a fork and salt as desired.

TYPES OF BROWN RICE

BROWN LONG GRAIN: the most common grain that can be cooked as suggested above and used in salads, stews or bakes for a quick shot of energy on the run.

BROWN BASMATI: has the same nutty aroma as white basmati, with more chew.

BROWN SHORT GRAIN: this is a squishier grain that can be cooked up into a creamy stew for breakfast or a late night snack when burning the midnight oil.

BROWN RICE HAS A SECRET

Brown rice flour is a lesser known tip for home cooks who love battering and frying: instead of using white flour for the next home batch of battered fish, try brown rice flour, which is gluten free and rich in protein. Brown rice flour is also excellent for thickening sauces and baking into cakes and biscuits — brown rice and chocolate chips go together like peanuts and butter.

Crispy Tofu Mango Salad

THIS SALAD HAS IT ALL: SWEET MANGO, TANGY LIME, CRUNCHY BEANS AND ENERGY - BOOSTING NUTS AND TOFU

SERVES 4

TOFU

400g (14oz) firm tofu

¼ tsp salt

3 tbsps cornflour

2 tbsps vegetable oil

GLAZE

1 lime, finely zested, then juiced

¼ cup (90g, 3oz) maple syrup

½ tbsp soy sauce

1 tsp cornflour

SALAD

1 cup (165g, 6oz) cooked wild rice

1 mango, peeled and cut into small cubes

½ Lebanese cucumber, halved lengthways and sliced

200g (7oz) snow peas, ends trimmed and thinly sliced

1 small red onion, finely chopped

Pinch of red pepper flakes

2 tbsps fresh coriander, finely chopped

½ cup (60g, 2oz) fresh cashews or peanuts, chopped

Firstly you need to remove as much moisture as you can from the tofu. Line a plate with about 4 folded paper towels and place the block of tofu on top. Place another plate over the tofu and weigh it down with a large can or even a pot full of water. Let the tofu sit for at least 20 minutes or longer. Pat the tofu dry after this and cut into cubes.

In a medium bowl gently toss the tofu cubes with the salt and the cornflour, ensuring the cubes are evenly coated with the flour.

In a large bowl, mix together all the salad ingredients except the rice and put aside.

In a small bowl, mix together ½ teaspoon lime zest, all the lime juice, maple syrup, soy sauce and cornflour. Stir to dissolve the cornflour. Set aside.

In a large frying pan, heat the oil over medium-high heat. Add the tofu to the pan in a single layer. If the tofu doesn't start to sizzle as soon as you place it in the pan, the oil needs to be heated further. Fry the tofu for about 3 minutes on each side — it should be browned and easy to turn when it's cooked. Once cooked, remove the tofu and turn down the heat.

Add the glaze mixture to the pan, giving it a quick stir first to ensure the conflour is still mixed through. Heat it until it just begins to simmer and thicken. As soon as it thickens, pour it over the salad ingredients in the bowl and toss to coat.

Add the cooked wild rice and tofu to the bowl and gently stir to combine.

Season to taste with salt and pepper.

Spiced Mushroom Risotto

BREAK WITH TRADITION AND SUBSTITUTE BROWN RICE FOR ARBORIO TO GIVE YOUR RISOTTO A HEALTHFUL BOOST

SERVES 2

2 tbsps butter

2 tbsps olive oil

1 small onion, finely chopped

2 cloves garlic, minced

1 tsp turmeric

½ tsp ground cumin

1½ cups (235g, 7oz) brown rice (short grain if possible)

½ cup (125ml, 4fl oz) dry white wine (such as Sauvignon Blanc)

300g (10oz) button mushrooms, sliced

4 cups (1L, 2pt) hot vegetable stock

3 tbsps sour cream

¼ cup (30g, 1oz) Parmesan cheese, grated

Salt and pepper, to taste

¼ cup (10g, ¼ oz) fresh parsley, chopped

In a large, heavy-based saucepan, heat the butter and oil over medium-high heat. Add the onion and cook for 5 minutes. Add the garlic, turmeric and cumin and stir for 1 minute until fragrant. Stir in the rice and cook for another minute.

Add the wine and cook until is has been soaked up completely by the rice. Add the mushrooms and stir for 2 minutes.

Add the vegetable stock, roughly ⅔ cup at a time. Stir the rice each time until all the stock has been completely absorbed.

The rice grains should be nice and soft.

Remove the saucepan from the heat and stir through the sour cream and cheese. Season to taste with salt and pepper.

Garnish with chopped parsley.

Brown and Red Rice Bowl

EARTHY AND NUTTY IN FLAVOUR, THIS HEARTY BOWL IS FULL OF GOOD VIBES AND GOOD NUTRIENTS

SERVES 4

1 tbsps olive oil

1 onion, chopped

1 cup (155g, 4oz) red rice

1 cup (155g, 4oz) brown rice

4 cups (1L, 2pt) vegetable stock

¼ cup (60g, 2oz) tomato paste

¼ tsp salt

1½ cups (50g, 2oz) green beans

¼ cup (10g, ¼ oz) fresh basil, chopped

Salt and pepper, to taste

Heat the oil in a large frying pan over a medium-high heat. Add the onion and fry for 4-5 minutes, stirring, until soft.

Add the red rice and the brown rice and stir for a minute or two, then add a splash of the stock. Fry until evapourated, then reduce the heat to medium.

Add the tomato paste, stir, and pour in a little more of the stock (about a quarter of it). Allow the rice to cook for 5 minutes, stirring occasionally.

Add another quarter of the stock, and the beans, stir, and allow to cook for a further 5 minutes.

Add the remainder of the stock and cook for 10 minutes until rice is tender. If the mixture is too thick and rice is not yet cooked, add a little water as required until the rice is tender and the mixture is creamy.

Season to taste with salt and pepper. Stir through the fresh basil just before serving.

Barley Bean Salad

SERVES 4

¼ tsp salt

½ cup (95g, 3oz) pearl barley, rinsed and drained

250g (9oz) green beans, ends trimmed

4 spring onions, finely chopped

¼ cup (10g, ¼ oz) dill, chopped

3 tbsps olive oil

2 tbsps lemon juice

2 tbsps white wine vinegar

Salt and pepper, to taste

In a medium-sized saucepan, bring 1 litre of water and the salt to a boil. Add the barley and simmer for 30 minutes until tender. Drain and set aside to cool.

Steam the beans over a simmering pot for 5 minutes until the beans are tender. Don't let them get too soft.

To assemble the salad, mix together in a large salad bowl the barley, beans, spring onions and dill.

In a small bowl, whisk together the olive oil, lemon juice, vinegar and some salt and pepper. Pour over the salad and toss to combine. Season to taste and serve.

Green Bean Salad

SERVES 4

900g (2lb) fresh green beans, washed and trimmed

3 tbsps olive oil

½ cup (60g, 2oz) slivered almonds

2 cloves garlic, minced

1 red capsicum, finely sliced

Salt and pepper, to taste

In a large saucepan, boil the beans in water with a pinch of salt for 3 minutes. Drain and rinse with cold water. Set aside.

In a medium-sized saucepan heat 1 tablespoon of the oil over medium heat. Add the almonds and fry, stirring constantly, for 2 minutes until the almonds start to brown. Immediately remove the almonds from the pan and set aside to cool.

Heat the rest of the oil in the frying pan and add the garlic and capsicum. Cook for 2 minutes then add the beans and fry for a further 3 minutes. The beans should be slightly browned from the frying.

To serve, toss the almonds through the beans and capsicum. Season to taste.

GREEN BEANS

The green bean comes in many disguises. Although the beans inside a green bean are always green, the pods can be green, gold, purple, red or streaked. This speaks to the stability and the versatility of this crunchy, zesty vegetable, a bag of which could make a week of snacks at the office or on the beach. The French revere them, simply steamed and covered in butter and salt. All their colour variations make a surprising salad, dressed with lemon and oil. And they are also excellent support for crumbles of feta or blue cheese.

Lemon Herb-Crusted Chicken Breast

THIS MEDITERRANEAN-STYLE CHICKEN DISH IS A LOVELY DINNER OPTION THAT CAN BE SERVED WITH SALAD OR VEGETABLES

SERVES 6

1½ cups (185g, 6oz) breadcrumbs

3 tbsps Parmesan cheese, grated

2 tbsps mixed herbs

1 tbsp fresh parsley, finely chopped

1 tsp fresh thyme, finely chopped

1 tbsp lemon zest

¾ cup (90g, 3oz) plain flour

Salt and pepper

6 small chicken breasts, skin removed

3 large eggs, beaten

1 lemon, cut into 6 wedges

Preheat oven to 180°C (350°F, Gas Mark 4) and line a flat baking tray with baking paper.

In a shallow bowl, mix together the breadcrumbs, Parmesan, herbs and lemon zest.

In a separate shallow bowl, mix the flour with a good pinch each of salt and pepper.

Pat dry the chicken breasts and then lightly coat each breast with the seasoned flour, dip in the beaten egg, then coat thoroughly in the breadcrumbs. Shake off any excess flour, egg or breadcrumbs at each step.

Place each completed crumbed breast on the tray in a single layer.

Place the tray in the oven and bake for 20 minutes until the crust is nice and browned.

Serve with wedges of lemon and a side salad.

Chargrilled Chicken Legs

A FLAVOUR-FILLED TREAT THAT TAKES FIVE MINUTES TO PREPARE
AND MAKES A GREAT DINNER WITH FRESH SALAD ON THE SIDE

SERVES 6

6 chicken drumsticks

¼ cup (60ml, 2fl oz) olive oil

4 cloves garlic, minced

1 tsp tomato paste

1 tbsp smoked paprika

¼ tsp cayenne pepper

1 tsp fresh thyme, finely chopped

1 tbsp fresh oregano, chopped

1 tbsp lemon juice

Salt and pepper, to taste

Pat dry the drumsticks and set aside.

In a large bowl, combine all the other ingredients together thoroughly.

Toss the drumsticks in the marinade to coat them completely.

Heat a large grill pan to high heat. Lay the drumsticks in a single layer without letting them touch each other (you may need to do this in two batches — don't overcrowd them). Grill the legs for 5 minutes each side or until they start to get one or two scorch marks.

Serve with fresh salad ingredients and lime wedges.

BRUSSELS SPROUTS

Brussels sprouts are loved or loathed. If you are in the latter camp, consider trying again because these crunchy little balls have unique health benefits. They're high in protein and iron, so are amazing for muscle building and repair and for 24-hour energy. They're also as high in vitamin C as most red berries.

Still not keen? Consider this: it's all in the way they are cooked. Boiled and soggy does nothing for their reputation. But there are so many ways to make Brussels sprouts delicious and to even hide the flavour while the taste buds adjust.

BRUSSELS SPROUTS IN SO MANY WAYS

BRUSSELS SPROUTS GRATIN: A healthier version of the classic potato dish in which whole sprouts are baked in cream, Parmesan cheese and thyme.

BRUSSELS SPROUTS ROASTED WITH GARLIC AND CHILLI: One trick to roasting these dense vegetable balls is to pan-fry them for a few minutes first until they brown on the bottom. Then add cloves of garlic and roast for 15 minutes, shaking them every few minutes. (First: chop the bottoms off the vegetables and cut them in half.)

SAUTEED BRUSSELS SPROUTS WITH RED ONION AND FETA: After 8 to 10 minutes in a pan with some olive oil, they become soft and sweet as they caramelize. The onion can be thrown in early for more sweetness or at the last minute for a tart, savory effect. Sprinkle the feta over once in a bowl.

RAW IN A SALAD: They have a peppery taste and are softer than raw cabbage when soaked in water. Add nuts and Parmesan cheese and don't be shy with a dressing of lots of olive oil, salt, pepper and chives.

STEAMED BRUSSELS SPROUTS WITH BUTTER: A steaming basket is a great purchase for vegetable lovers — it's a foldable metal colander that sits on top or inside a saucepan above boiling water. Brussels sprouts only need 8 to 10 minutes before they become an even more vibrant green and retain their crunchiness for eating. Butter and lots of cracked pepper will do the trick here.

TIPS FOR SHOPPING AND PREPPING

- Choose the buds that have tightly closed, green leaves. Avoid signs of yellowing, which means they are ageing. Also avoid a cabbage-y smell — they should smell more like freshly cut grass.
- To clean dirt from inside the leaves, trim the ends and rinse for many minutes in a large bowl of cold water. Transfer to a colander and pat dry.
- Store them in the crisper or vegetable drawer of the fridge. They can stay fresh for up to a week and a half, which is longer than many green vegetables.

Sweet and Sour Sauteed Sprouts

IF YOU WANT TO LOVE SPROUTS BUT DON'T KNOW HOW, HERE'S HOW: FRY THEM UP WITH EARTHY MUSHROOMS AND TANGY CRANBERRIES

SERVES 4

500g (1lb) Brussels sprouts

2 tbsps olive oil

200g (7oz) thick cut bacon, fat trimmed and chopped

500g (1lb) shiitake mushrooms, sliced

½ cup (125ml, 4fl oz) chicken stock

2 tbsps soy sauce

2 tsps balsamic vinegar

1 tsp Dijon mustard

¼ cup (30g, 1oz) dried cranberries

Salt and pepper to taste

Wash Brussels sprouts. Trim the ends and remove any discoloured leaves and cut in half lengthways.

Heat 1 tablespoon oil in a large frying pan over medium-high heat. Add the bacon and fry for 4 minutes, until the bacon begins to crisp. Add the rest of the oil and then add the Brussels sprouts. Cook them through for 5 minutes until they begin to brown. Add the mushrooms and fry for 1 minute. Add the stock, soy sauce, vinegar and mustard. Cook until most of the liquid has evaporated, then remove from heat.

Stir through the cranberries and season to taste.

Serve.

Pork Schnitzel

SERVES 2-4

2 cups (250g, 8oz) breadcrumbs

1 clove garlic, minced

1 tbsp fresh sage, finely chopped

1 tbsp fresh parsley, finely chopped

1 tsp paprika

½ cup (60g, 2oz) plain flour

Salt and freshly ground black pepper

700g (1½ lb) boneless pork chops, 1cm (½ in) thick

3 medium eggs, beaten

¼ cup (60ml, 2fl oz) canola or vegetable oil (for frying)

In a shallow bowl, mix together the breadcrumbs, garlic, herbs and paprika. In a separate shallow bowl, mix the flour with a good pinch each of salt and pepper.

To coat the chops, lightly cover each one with flour, dip in the beaten egg, then coat in breadcrumbs.

Heat up half the oil in a large frying pan. Fry pork in batches, two at a time, for 3 minutes on each side. Add more of the oil as needed for each batch. The chops should be browned and crisp all over. Place the schnitzels onto paper towels once cooked to help soak up excess oil.

Sweet Brussels Sprout Salad

SERVES 2-4

500g (1lb 2oz) Brussels sprouts, trimmed and halved

1 cup (100g, 3½ oz) red seedless grapes

1 tbsp olive oil

1 tsp lemon zest

1 tsp thyme, finely chopped

½ cup (60g, 2oz) walnuts

DRESSING

1 spring onion, finely chopped

2 tsps Dijon mustard

2 tbsps of balsamic vinegar

¼ cup (60ml, 2fl oz) olive oil (roughly)

Salt and pepper to taste

Preheat oven to 200°C (400°F, Gas Mark 6). In a bowl, toss sprouts and grapes with olive oil, lemon zest and thyme. Line a large baking dish with baking paper. Scatter sprouts and grapes in the dish and roast in the oven for 25 minutes. In a small bowl, whisk together the spring onion, mustard, vinegar, oil, salt and pepper. Place cooked sprouts and grapes into a bowl. Add the walnuts. Pour over the dressing and mix thoroughly.

CAPERS

They might be the world's tastiest flower buds — smaller than a green pea and with more flavour than an onion. Usually, they're sold in jars, marinating in a light vinegar brine, and their role is to add bursts of flavour and texture to salads or a sandwich that's missing a little something. They are a source of iron, fibre and vitamin K, which helps prevent blood clotting and is essential in the healing of injuries. Recently their older sisters, caperberries, have made splashes — caperberries are even more pungent and herby tasting and can be eaten in a mouthful like a cherry tomato.

PORK

Pork has been branded 'the other white meat' because it can be very lean and it is also full of iron. The slogan has been debated, as everyone knows that part of the appeal of bacon or a succulent chunk of pork belly is the fat that lines it, which can be so beautifully salty and crunchy when cooked right.

Pork fat is special occasion stuff. The flesh of the piggy is low in fat, nutritious and very tasty. Runners and tradesmen who work long hours in the sun can thrive on a meal of pork chops and broccoli.

IT'S ALL IN THE CUT

Head to the butcher and ask for tenderloin, loin chops or a sirloin roast. Half of all of these cuts are protein and the rest is flowing with essential B vitamins like B12, thiamin and niacin, which are great for the immune system and metabolism. A 100g portion has about 16% of the recommended daily value of both protein and these B vitamins.

WHY BUY LOCAL

This is a golden age in the food world for the words organic, sustainable, local. Some say it's all marketing. Other experts have done research into determining whether 'organic' and 'sustainable' makes a difference. If organic, locally raised pork is available, it may be the healthiest option. The more local a piece of pork, the cleaner the meat — commercial pig farms are likely to use antibiotics that smaller farms don't need to use to keep their pigs healthy. These antibiotics are not the best for keeping the liver and kidneys happy, which means the body works harder to get rid of toxins and excess nutrients. If the organs are working harder, there will be more yawning and less motivation for weekend adventures and new life experiences.

TRICKS FOR COOKING PORK

Pork chops are big and juicy. That is until they are overcooked and land on the plate with a 'thud'. Dry pork chops aren't so tasty and are harder to digest.

Marinades are part of the answer: a simple marinade of honey, soy sauce, a splash of sesame or olive oil and maybe ginger or garlic is great for baking pork tenderloins or pork chops. Baking is the easiest method for cooking the meat evenly all the way through. A barbecue or a saucepan is great for a crispy outside, so long as the heat is kept moderate and the meat moistened by the marinade.

A way to avoid the uneven cook is to buy thinner pork chops — they are packaged in most supermarket meat sections or a local butcher will usually happily advise and tailor a chop to individual likings.

Classic Pork Tenderloin

A LOW-FAT AND HIGH-COMFORT ALTERNATIVE TO THE TRADITIONAL SUNDAY ROAST

SERVES 6

750g (1½ lb) pork tenderloin

1 tsp salt

Freshly ground black pepper

2 cloves garlic, minced

1 tbsp fresh sage, finely chopped

½ tsp ground coriander

½ tsp ground cumin

1 tsp Dijon mustard

3 tbsps olive oil

6 small wooden skewers, soaked in hot water for at least 30 minutes.

1 lemon, cut into 6 wedges

Preheat oven to 200°C (400°F, Gas Mark 6).

Trim tenderloin of silver skin and fat. Pierce the loin all over with a fork.

In a small bowl, mix together the salt, a couple of grinds of pepper, garlic, sage, coriander, cumin, mustard and 2 tablespoons of the oil. Coat the loin with the paste, rubbing it right into the meat.

In a large, heavy frying pan, heat the rest of the olive oil over high heat. Place the tenderloin in the pan and brown it evenly on all sides. This should take you 6 minutes in total.

Insert the wooden skewers evenly along the length of the loin fillet and place in a large baking dish in the oven and roast for 15 minutes. Turn the meat over after 7 minutes. Remove from the oven and let it sit for 10 minutes.

Cut the fillet into 6 even slices, each slice should have one skewer sitting in the middle.

Serve each skewer with a lemon wedge.

Pork Stir-Fry

THIS FRESH, EASY, FEEL-GOOD STIR-FRY IS THE PERFECT
SCHOOL-NIGHT SUPPER

SERVES 4

750g (1½ lb) pork
tenderloin

1 tbsp honey

2 tbsps soy sauce

1 tsp five-spice powder

2 tbsps brown sugar

1 tsp chilli powder

1 cloves garlic, chopped

1 tsp sesame oil

300g (10oz) rice
noodles

1 tbsp peanut (or other
neutral) oil

1 carrot, julienned

2 spring onions, sliced

1 capsicum, seeded and
sliced

1 small zucchini, sliced

150g (5oz) snow peas,
sliced lengthwise

3 kaffir lime leaves,
finely shredded

2 tbsps orange juice

2 tbsps sesame seeds

Slice the pork into pieces — thick enough to be substantial
but thin enough to cook through quickly. Tenderloin is a lean
and tender cut but marinating will improve it. In a large bowl,
combine the honey, soy sauce, five-spice, sugar, chilli, garlic and
sesame oil. Add the pork and gently turn to coat it in marinade,
then cover the bowl and place in the fridge for a minimum of 3
hours and overnight if time allows.

Cook noodles according to the instructions on the packet. Drain
and cover to keep warm. Set aside.

Remove the pork from the fridge and shake off excess marinade.
Retain the marinade to use in cooking later. Heat the peanut oil
in a wok. Stir-fry the pork in batches according to the size of
your wok until browned. Set aside.

Stir-fry the carrot, spring onion and capsicum for 2-3 minutes
until softened. Add pork and stir-fry for a further 3-4 minutes
until pork is cooked. Add the zucchini, snow peas, kaffir lime
leaves and retained marinade and orange juice, and stir-fry until
snow peas are tender but still crisp. Remove from heat, then add
sesame seeds, and noodles. Gently toss to combine, then transfer
to bowls to serve.

Baked Ricotta Shells with Tomato Sauce

AN ENERGY-BOOSTING DINNER THAT'S GREAT FOR THE NIGHT BEFORE A WORKOUT OR RUN

SERVES 2

20 jumbo pasta shells

TOMATO SAUCE

¼ cup (60ml, 2fl oz) extra virgin olive oil

1 tsp red chilli flakes

½ tsp sea salt

3 cloves garlic, finely chopped

2 x 400g (14oz) cans crushed tomatoes

Zest of 1 lemon

FILLING

2 tbsps olive oil

2 cloves garlic, minced

1 bunch fresh spinach, leaves picked and chopped

340g (12oz) ricotta cheese

1 cup (125g, 4oz) mozzarella cheese, grated

½ cup (60g, 2oz) Parmesan cheese, shaved

1 egg

1 tbsp fresh basil, chopped

1 tsp salt

½ tsp pepper

Parmesan and fresh pepper, to serve

Preheat the oven to 190°C (375°F, Gas Mark 5).

Bring a large saucepan of salted water to the boil. Add pasta and cook until almost al dente. Drain and set aside.

Meanwhile, make the sauce. Combine the olive oil, red chilli flakes, sea salt and garlic in a saucepan over medium-high heat, saute just 45 seconds or so until everything is fragrant — don't let the garlic brown. Stir in the tomatoes and heat to a gentle simmer. Season with salt and stir in the lemon zest.

Meanwhile, heat the olive oil in a large frying pan over a medium-high heat. Add the garlic and cook for 1-2 minutes, until golden. Add the spinach and cook for a further 1-2 minutes, stirring occasionally, until the leaves begin to wilt but are still bright green. Set aside to cool.

In a large bowl, mix the spinach, ricotta, mozzarella, Parmesan, egg, basil and salt and pepper until thoroughly combined.

Pour half of the tomato sauce into the bottom of a baking dish.

Stuff each pasta shell with the spinach and ricotta filling, and place in the baking dish.

Cover with the remaining sauce and bake, covered, for 25 minutes. Serve warm with a dusting of Parmesan and plenty of freshly ground pepper.

Lamb Kebabs with Yoghurt Sauce

THESE DELICIOUS, MIDDLE-EASTERN-STYLE KEBABS PROVIDE A NICE BALANCE OF FLAVOURS AND NUTRIENTS FOR DINNER

SERVES 4

2 tbsps olive oil

1 tbsp thyme, finely chopped

1 tbsp fresh oregano, finely chopped

1 tbsp rosemary, finely chopped

2 cloves garlic, minced

Salt and pepper, to taste

700g (1 ½ lb) lamb mince

2 tbsps vegetable oil

8 wooden skewers, soaked in hot water for at least 30 minutes

4 pita breads

4 leaves butter lettuce

1 red onion, quartered and finely sliced

Seeds from 1 pomegranate

YOGHURT DIPPING SAUCE

1 cup (225g, 8oz) Greek yoghurt

1 clove garlic, minced

1 tsp fresh mint, finely chopped

Salt and pepper, to taste

1 tsp fresh parsley, chopped

In a small bowl, whisk together the oil, thyme, oregano, rosemary and garlic, along with a good couple of grinds of salt and pepper.

In a large bowl, mix together the lamb mince and the herb mixture until thoroughly combined. Use your hands to split the mixture into 8 equal portions.

Mould the lamb mixture onto skewers into small sausage shapes. Season with salt and pepper.

Heat a grill pan or barbecue grill to high heat. Lightly brush the lamb with the vegetable oil. Grill each kebab for 4 minutes on each of their four sides.

To make the yoghurt sauce, in a medium bowl, mix together the yoghurt, garlic and mint and add salt and pepper to taste. Place into a small dip bowl and sprinkle over a tablespoon of pomegranate seeds and chopped parsley.

To serve, on top of a flat pita bread place a lettuce leaf, sprinkle over some of the red onion and 2 tablespoons pomegranate seeds. Place 2 kebabs on top and serve with a side of dipping sauce.

Tom Yum Soup

THIS CLASSIC THAI SOUP WILL LEAVE YOUR TOES HOPPING AND TASTEBUDS TINGLING

SERVES 6

2 cups (500ml, 1pt) chicken stock

1 stalk lemongrass, sliced

Small piece galangal or ginger, very thinly sliced

6-7 kaffir lime leaves, torn

170g (6oz) fresh button or oyster mushrooms, chopped

2 tbsps nam prik pao (Thai chilli paste)

¼ cup (60ml, 2fl oz) fish sauce

4-5 fresh red bird's-eye chillies, crushed

24 jumbo prawns, peeled and deveined, with the head and tail sections intact

1 cup (250ml, 8fl oz) coconut milk

1 lime, juiced, to taste

Fish sauce, to taste

¼ cup (5g, ¼ oz) lightly packed coriander leaves

In a medium saucepan, bring the stock to a gentle boil over a medium heat, then immediately reduce the heat so that the liquid is just simmering. Add the lemongrass, galangal or ginger, and kaffir lime leaves. Next add the mushrooms and stir in the nam prik pao. Add the fish sauce, followed by the crushed chillies.

As the soup is simmering, gently drop the prawns into it. Turn up the heat a small amount to keep the soup at a steady simmer. Cook for about 1 minute, stirring occasionally, until the prawns have firmed up slightly.

Add the coconut milk and cook until simmering again and then remove from the heat. Season soup with lime juice and fish sauce to taste.

Stir in coriander leaves and serve.

PRAWNS

Isn't it fun when the most luxurious foods to eat are also the treats that will keep us moving. A prawn cocktail for lunch or afternoon tea might sound fancy but it's easy to prepare, low in calories and gives a major shot of lean protein. Prawns are full of zinc, vitamin E and iron — one prawn could compete with a bowl of spinach — so excellent as a snack to cruise through the afternoon slump.

BUY THE BEST

- Fresh prawns, whether raw or cooked, should smell salty, not fishy.
- They should have a nice shiny outer and not look dry, which means they are past their prime or have been frozen and defrosted and lost their nutrients.
- Generally fresh, uncooked prawns will be anything from translucent to a bluish grey. Stay away from prawns that are inconsistently coloured in the head or shell, as this can suggest the flesh is starting to go off.
- Avoid any that have broken or cracked shells.
- Frozen prawns are just as good as fresh. Most brands have been flash frozen and retain nutrients for months in the freezer. Look for 'IQF' somewhere on the bag — that means individually quick frozen, which is the method for keeping them from sticking together in the freezer.

PRAWN PREPARATION

For the simplest, juiciest prawns:
- Run the cold tap over fresh or defrosted prawns in a big bowl. (Always defrost prawns before cooking.)
- Prepare a salted ice bath for later: add salt to a large bowl of water and three handfuls of ice.
- Throw the prawns into a bowl or saucepan of boiling water and watch them turn pink. It'll take one or two minutes.
- Transfer cooked prawns to the ice bath. A slotted spoon is best, to keep the boiling water from the fresh ice. See the pink morph to a sunset orange.
- Once the prawns are cooled, pull the shell up and around the body. Pinch the tail and give it a twist to remove it.
- Use a small, sharp knife with a curved blade to make a shallow incision along the back from head to just above the tail; remove and discard vein.

SHELF LIFE

- Like all shellfish, prawns go off quickly. Keep in the fridge wrapped in their original packaging or in a sealed container. Eat within 24 hours of purchase.
- Frozen prawns keep for between 3 and 6 months.

Vietnamese Prawn Noodle Salad

AN AUTHENTIC VIETNAMESE DISH, THIS SATISFYING AND REFRESHING PRAWN SALAD IS WELL WORTH THE EFFORT

SERVES 4

¼ cup (20g, ¾ oz) soya beans

200g (7oz) flat rice noodles

1 tsp sesame oil

1 cup (90g, 3oz) red cabbage, shredded

1 cup (90g, 3oz) Chinese cabbage (wombok), shredded

1 bunch bok choy, ends trimmed and sliced

500g (1lb 2oz) fresh green prawns, deveined and shelled

3 small red radishes, sliced

2 spring onions, thinly sliced

1 small Lebanese cucumber, thinly sliced

½ bunch coriander leaves

2 tbsps white and black sesame seeds, to garnish

DRESSING

1 clove garlic, minced

2 tsps sesame oil

2 tsps brown sugar

4 tbsps lime juice

2 tbsps soy sauce

2 tbsps fish sauce

1 tbsp fresh ginger, grated

¼ cup (60ml, 2fl oz) rice wine vinegar

¼ cup (60ml, 2fl oz) water

To make the dressing, in a medium bowl whisk together all the dressing ingredients. Set aside.

In a small bowl, cover the soya beans with boiling water and let soak until they're softened, at least 15 minutes, then drain.

In a medium pot, bring a litre of water to the boil and cook the rice noodles according the packet instructions. Drain, then rinse with cold water. Place in a bowl and stir through the sesame oil to prevent the noodles from sticking to each other.

Using a steamer, steam the cabbages and bok choy for 4 minutes until softened but still slightly crisp. Remove and place in a large bowl.

Steam the prawns for 8 minutes until they turn pink-orange. Remove and add to the cabbage mix.

Add the rest of the salad ingredients to the bowl, excluding the noodles, and mix thoroughly.

Gently stir through the noodles and half of the dressing. Add more dressing to taste.

Serve chilled, garnished with sesame seeds.

Salmon Cakes

SERVES 2

4 medium potatoes, peeled and chopped

225g (8oz) can salmon

1 tbsp capers

1 tbsp chopped chives

Salt and pepper, to season

2 eggs, beaten

½ cup (60g, 2oz) breadcrumbs

1 tbsp olive oil

Sour cream and fresh dill, to serve

Place potatoes in a large saucepan of salted water and bring to the boil. Cook for 10 minutes, until tender. Drain and return to the pan. Roughly mash then place in a large bowl and cool slightly. Add salmon, capers and chives, and stir to combine. Season with salt and pepper. Gradually add half the beaten egg to bring the mixture together. Using your hands, form mixture into patties. Place remaining egg in one bowl and breadcrumbs in another. Dip each patty into the egg, then breadcrumbs. Heat the oil in a frying pan. Add the salmon cakes, and cook for 5 minutes on each side until golden and crispy.

Prawn and Pesto Pasta

SERVES 6

500g (1lb 2oz) penne pasta

¼ cup (60ml, 2fl oz) olive oil

5 cloves garlic, minced

½ cup (60g, 2oz) pine nuts

½ cup (20g, ¾ oz) fresh basil, finely chopped

750g (1½ lb) fresh prawns, peeled and deveined

1 tbsp mint, finely chopped

1 tbsp oregano, finely chopped

1 cup (125g, 4oz) Parmesan cheese; grated

Salt and pepper, to taste

In a large pot, bring 2 litres of salted water to a boil and cook the penne until al dente. Drain, reserving ½ cup of the cooking liquid. Set pasta and reserved liquid aside. In a large, deep-sided frying pan, heat 3 tablespoons of the oil over a medium-high heat. Add garlic, pine nuts and 2 tablespoons of the basil and cook for 2 minutes. Add prawns, mint and oregano and fry until prawns are cooked and pink. Turn heat to low and add the penne, the rest of the oil and reserved pasta liquid to the pan. Gently heat through. Remove from heat and stir through remaining basil and cheese. Season to taste.

PINE NUTS

Pine nuts are a bit of a luxury — smooth teardrops bursting with protein, iron and good fat for a healthy heart. Toasted pine nuts add a scrumptious buttery taste and salty crunch to salads and pastas. Their most famous role is as the heft in pesto, that chunky puree of pine nuts, basil, olive oil, lemon, salt and pepper, which can be stirred through a plate of buckwheat noodles or lathered over a pizza base for a lot of extra flavour and nutrients.

Asparagus and Prawn Bisque

THIS LUSCIOUS SOUP IS A MODERN TAKE ON AN OLD-FASHIONED FAVOURITE FROM THE SOUTHERN STATES OF THE USA

SERVES 6

1 tsp olive oil

3 cloves garlic, chopped

1 small brown onion, finely chopped

800g (1¾ lb) asparagus, woody ends trimmed

3 cups (750ml, 24fl oz) vegetable stock

¼ cup (10g, ¼ oz) plus 2 tbsps fresh parsley, roughly chopped

4 tsps lemon juice

1 cup (250ml, 8fl oz) coconut cream

12 fresh prawn tails, peeled and deveined

¼ tsp cayenne pepper

Salt and pepper, to taste

In a large pot, heat the olive oil over medium heat. Add the garlic and onion and gently fry for 4 minutes until the onion is softened.

Chop about three-quarters of the asparagus into roughly 3cm (1in) pieces.

Add the chopped asparagus to the pot and add enough stock to cover it completely. You need to hold at least ½ cup (125ml, 4fl oz) of stock in reserve. Cook the asparagus for 5 minutes, until it is tender and still a vivid green. Remove the pot from the heat and throw in the parsley and lemon juice. Let it cool slightly.

Pour the warm soup mix into a food processor or blender. Be careful not to fill it too much or it will explode all over your kitchen. Do it in batches if you need to. As you are blending the soup, gradually add the coconut cream.

Cut the remaining asparagus into half lengths. In your now empty pot, heat the reserved stock over medium heat and add the asparagus pieces. Cook them for 2 minutes or until they are tender and still a vivid green.

Pour the soup back into the pot with the asparagus pieces. Add the prawn tails and cayenne and heat until the prawns are cooked through.

Season to taste with salt and pepper and serve garnished with a sprinkling of chopped parsley.

Easy
Entertaining

Prosciutto Stuffed Chicken Breast with Cucumber Salad

THIS CLASSIC ITALIAN-INSPIRED CHICKEN SERVED WITH A FRESH SALAD ON THE SIDE IS A WELL-BALANCED DINNER FOR YOUR GUESTS

SERVES 6

2 large chicken breasts, skin removed

10 slices prosciutto

¼ tsp salt flakes

STUFFING

4 preserved artichoke hearts, rinsed and chopped

50g (2oz) sundried tomatoes, finely chopped

1 clove garlic, minced

1 tsp fresh marjoram, finely chopped

200g (7oz) camembert, straight from the fridge, cut into small cubes

1 tsp freshly cracked black pepper

½ tsp smoked paprika

SALAD

2 continental cucumbers

1 tsp soy sauce

3 tbsps white wine vinegar

1 tbsp caster sugar

1 tsp lemon juice

½ tbsp salt flakes

Fresh ground black pepper, to taste

Preheat oven to 190°C (375°F, Gas Mark 5).

In a medium bowl, prepare your stuffing by mixing together all the ingredients thoroughly. Set aside.

Cut into the breasts by placing them flat on your chopping board and putting your hand flat on the top. Insert the blade of your knife into the middle of the top corner of the breast and slice, bringing the blade down towards you and cutting into the breast nearly all the way through. Stop cutting with about 2cm (1in) to spare at the bottom of the breast. You should then be able to 'butterfly' it open at the top. Place a piece of plastic wrap over the butterflied breast and gently bang it with a blunt object such as rolling pin to flatten until it's about 1cm (½ in) thick.

Line 5 slices of prosciutto under each other slightly overlapping to form a square. Place opened chicken breasts over these.

Divide the stuffing in half and place it in the centre of the flattened breasts. Use the ends of the prosciutto slices to help you roll up the chicken around the filling. Place the rolls on a baking tray, seam side down. Cover with foil and bake for 45 minutes, then remove the foil and bake for another 15 minutes or until the prosciutto is crispy. Remove from the oven and let sit for 10 minutes.

Using a vegetable shredder or spiraliser, peel the cucumber into long strips. Squeeze the strips as you go to remove excess moisture. In a small bowl, whisk together the rest of the salad ingredients. Add the dressing to the cucumber and mix through.

Thickly slice the chicken rolls and serve with the cucumber salad.

Salmon Mousse Tarts

THESE GORGEOUS LITTLE TARTS ARE WORTH EVERY SECOND YOU SPEND ON PREPARING THEM

SERVES 6

450g (1lb) raw salmon

½ cup (55g, 2oz) cream cheese, at room temperature

2 egg whites

1⅔ cups (400ml, 13fl oz) thickened cream

2 tbsps lemon juice

Tabasco sauce, to taste

170g (6oz) puff pastry sheets

1 egg, beaten, for glazing

Coarse salt

18 small prawns, deveined, tails removed

1 small Lebanese cucumber, halved lengthways and sliced

In a food processor or blender, puree the salmon and cream cheese. Add in the egg whites and blend again until thoroughly combined. Place in the fridge for 20 minutes to chill.

Remove from the fridge and mix through half of the cream, the lemon juice and a couple of drops of Tabasco. Put back in the fridge to chill.

Lightly whip the rest of the cream and gently fold into the salmon using a slotted spoon until thoroughly combined. Put back in the fridge for 15 minutes.

Preheat oven to 220°C (430°F, Gas Mark 7).

Using a 7cm (3in) diameter fluted biscuit or scone cutter, cut out as many circles as the pastry will allow. Gently fold up the edges with your fingers and place on a large flat baking tray lined with baking paper. Spoon or pipe the mousse filling into the tarts and brush the edges of the pastry with the beaten egg. Cool in the fridge again for 15 minutes then remove and bake in the oven for 30 minutes. Keep an eye on the tarts to ensure the pasty doesn't burn.

Remove from the oven and let them cool slightly.

Meanwhile, cook the prawns. In a medium-sized pot, bring 1 litre of salted water to the boil. Drop in the prawns and boil until they just start to colour. Immediately drain and rinse in cold water. Pat the prawns dry.

To assemble, sit one of the cucumber slices. Around the bottom of the cucumber, arrange 3 of the prawns.

Chicken Skewers and Mango Salsa

WARM SPICES, ZESTY LIME JUICE, DELICATE CHICKEN BREAST
AND FRUITY SALSA COMBINE TO CREATE A WINNER DINNER

SERVES 4

CHICKEN

4 tbsps olive oil

3 cloves garlic, minced

1 tsp cumin

1 tsp smoked paprika

2 tsps ground oregano

2 limes, juiced

4 small chicken breasts

2 limes, cut into wedges

16 large wooden skewers, soaked in hot water for 30 minutes

2 tbsps small basil leaves.

2 tbsps parsley, roughly chopped

SALSA

2 mangos, peeled and cubed

5 spring onions, finely chopped

½ small red chilli, deseeded and finely chopped

2 tbsps coriander, finely chopped

1 tsp chilli flakes

1 lime, juiced

To make the marinade, mix together the oil, garlic, cumin, paprika, oregano and lime juice. Slice the chicken breasts lengthways into strips roughly 3cm (1in)wide. Soak the chicken strips in the marinade for at least 1 hour.

Mix together all the salsa ingredients and set aside to let the flavours infuse.

Heat a grill pan or barbecue grill to medium-high heat.

Gently thread the chicken strips onto the skewers. Grill the skewers on all four sides for 3 minutes on each side, basting with leftover marinade.

Serve the skewers with the salsa and the wedges of lime.

Sesame Crusted Sushi Cube

MAKES 30 (APPROX)

1 cup (155g, 4oz) uncooked sushi rice or short grain rice

1¼ cups (310ml, 10fl oz) water

3 generous tbsps rice wine vinegar

2 tsps caster sugar

Pinch of salt

¼ cup (30g, 1oz) mixed black and white sesame seeds

100g (3½ oz) smoked salmon, sliced

½ small avocado, sliced

1 small jar red fish roe (optional)

Rinse the rice until the water runs clear. Place in a small pot with the water and bring to the boil. Reduce heat to low and cover the pot. Check the rice in 8 minutes, if there is no more water, the rice is ready. Rinse under cold water in a colander to cool it down. Place the rice in a medium bowl. Mix together the rice wine vinegar, sugar and salt and then stir them through the rice. Mould heaped dessertspoons of the rice into small cubes. Roll each cube in the sesame seed mix.

Slice the smoked salmon into small strips. Place an avocado slice on top of each cube and drape a slice of salmon over that. Top with red fish roe, if using.

Sweet Potato Chips

SERVES 2

2 large sweet potatoes

Olive oil, for brushing

Sea salt and ground pepper, to season

Preheat oven to 120°C (250°F, Gas Mark ½) and line a baking tray with baking paper.

Slice the potatoes as thinly as you can — thinner equals crisper.

Pat completely dry with paper towel. Drizzle over the olive oil then rub it in using your hands. Sprinkle with salt and pepper. Transfer to the tray, spreading out in one even layer.

Set on the bottom shelf in the oven and allow to slowly bake for 2 hours until crispy. Remove from the oven and set aside for a further 10 minutes to crisp up even more.

Sprinkle with salt and serve immediately.

MOJITO MAGIC

Guess what? Mojitos are Good For You. Not really, but how about this: Kombucha Mojito. Try it — switch the soda for kombucha and the processed sugar for organic cane sugar or a simple syrup (made at home from organic sugar) and stand on one leg while you drink it — go on! Kombucha — in case you don't know — is a fermented, effervescent sweetened black tea that is hailed by some as the 'elixir of life' for its great health and detoxification benefits. It's widely available pre-made in stores these days.

Salmon Rolls

AN IMPRESSIVE, MELT-IN-THE-MOUTH LITTLE ENTREE THAT LOOKS A LOT HARDER TO MAKE THAN IT IS

SERVES 4

PANCAKE

1 tsp olive oil

1 clove garlic, minced

700g (1½ lb) fresh spinach leaves, chopped

2 tbsp flour

4 eggs, separated

FILLING

200g (7oz) cream cheese at room temperature

200g (7oz) smoked salmon slices

Preheat the oven to 200°C (400°F, Gas Mark 6). Line a large flat baking tray with baking paper.

In a pan heat the olive oil and cook the garlic for 1 minute. Add the spinach in handfulls until wilted. Remove from the heat, drain and pat dry with paper towels, then chop finely. Whisk the egg yolks through the spinach mixture. Add the flour and mix to combine. Set aside.

In a large bowl, beat the egg whites until stiff peaks form. Add the chopped spinach mixture. Lightly spread out the spinach mixture on the baking paper in the shape of a long rectangle.

Transfer to the oven to bake for 15 minutes until the pancake feels firm. After removing, roll up the pancake with the paper still inside along the long edge and let sit for 10 minutes.

Mash up the cream cheese until soft.

Unwrap the roll and spread the cream cheese in an even layer over it. Layer the slices of salmon on top of the cream cheese. Use the baking paper to help roll the spinach pancake up like a Swiss roll. Don't leave the paper inside it this time.

Place in the fridge overnight and slice into pieces before serving.

RAW FISH

Sushi these days can be both a luxurious treat and an everyday meal — award-winning restaurants and adventurous home chefs alike can buy fish that has been prepared and cut for a sushi feast. Sushi or raw fish is a brilliant choice before a night out dancing or in the days leading up to a camping trip. It is full of vitamins and healthy fat — the omega-3 fats are almost visible. These 'good fats' helps keep the heart healthy and skin supple, may protect against heart attacks and stroke, and are what the term 'brain food' refers to — they build cell membranes in the brain. Yet, while sushi has become a staple, it can be daunting to both order and prepare. There are a few rules to be aware of and handy tips to help out.

A FEW BASICS FOR THE BEGINNER

Even sushi lovers forget the difference in names for the most regular sushi categories:

MAKI: The most common rolls of rice wrapped in seaweed and filled with raw fish.

NIGIRI: A slice of raw fish draped over a bite-size bundle of rice.

SASHIMI: Raw fish, sliced into a rectangle and served with ginger and wasabi for taste. No rice.

THE FISH TO KNOW

TUNA: Tuna has a texture more delicate than red meat, yet a meatier flavour than other raw fish. A small tuna steak contains half the daily requirement of protein and essential amino acids. Not only will it keep you moving, this protein boosts the immune system.

SALMON: This is a lightly sweet fish with an elegant, creamy texture. Eaten raw, it almost melts on the tongue and can leave a lemony aftertaste.

KINGFISH: This pretty white fish has streaks and spots of reddish-pink. It has a creamy, lemony flavour and blends well with avocado, mango, cucumber or just eaten alone followed by a piece of pickled ginger, the condiment that is served with any plate in a Japanese restaurant along with wasabi and ginger.

TIPS FOR THE BRAVE HOME CHEF

- Ask for sashimi-grade selections.
- Use your nose: anything that smells fishy rather than salty should be avoided.
- Don't be tempted by the fluorescent — or at least oddly vibrant colours. A trick that farms use is to add colour to make the fish look more appealing.

Hawaiian Tuna Poke

THIS TROPICAL TWIST ON A RAW FISH DISH IS FULL OF FUN, FLAVOUR AND HIGH-ENERGY FOODS

SERVES 4

350g (12oz) raw sashimi-grade tuna, cut into 2cm (1in) cubes

1 tsp white sesame seeds

4 tsps tamari

2 tsps sesame oil

1 tsp honey

Pinch of sea salt

1 avocado, cubed

½ mango, cubed

½ white onion, chopped

TO SERVE

Handful coriander

1 tbsp black sesame seeds

1 tbsp white sesame seeds

Place the tuna in a bowl and add sesame seeds, tamari, sesame oil, honey and salt. Turn gently to coat the fish. Combine the avocado, mango and onion with the tuna. Taste and adjust seasonings as required.

Allow to sit at room temperature for 5-10 minutes before serving. To serve, divide onto four plates and press each serving into round mounds. Sprinkle sesame seeds over each dish and garnish with coriander.

Sesame Seared Tuna Tataki with Oyster Mushrooms

LIGHTLY SEARED TUNA MEETS CRISP STIR-FRIED VEGETABLES AND THE DELICATE FLAVOUR OF SESAME IN THIS SPECIAL DISH

SERVES 4

1 tsp salt flakes

400g (14oz) sashimi-grade tuna

1 tbsp vegetable oil

1 tbsp olive oil

2 tsps white sesame seeds

2 tsps black sesame seeds

1 tsp sesame oil

VEGETABLES

1 tbsp sesame oil

1 clove garlic, minced

½ cup (60g, 2oz) peanuts

400g (1lb) sugar snap peas, ends trimmed and sliced diagonally in half

4 heads baby bok choy, trimmed and thickly sliced on the diagonal

200g (8oz) oyster mushrooms, slice the larger mushrooms in half lengthways

2 spring onions, julienned into thin 4cm (1½ in) long strips

Soy sauce, to taste

Salt and pepper, to taste

NOTE: Prepare all ingredients before you start cooking. The tuna and vegetables need to be served as close as possible to cooking.

Sprinkle the salt over the tuna. Trim and slice the tuna into rectangular blocks around 10cm (4in) long and 5 x 3cm (2 x 1in) in width and height.

Mix the vegetable and olive oils in a small dish and lightly brush over the tuna slices.

Mix the white and black sesame seeds together on a small plate. Roll the tuna blocks in the sesame seeds, pressing so the seeds stick. In a medium frying pan, heat the sesame oil over medium heat. Sear the tuna quickly on all sides for 20 seconds each. Remove from the pan, slice into thin slices of about 1cm (½ in) and set aside.

Heat the sesame oil in a large wok on high heat. Add the garlic, peanuts, sugar snap peas and bok choy stems and stir fry for 1 minute. Add the bok choy leaves, mushrooms and spring onions. Stir for 2 more minutes. Add a splash or two of soy sauce if any moisture is needed. Remove from heat and season with salt and pepper. Then serve immediately with the tuna.

MUSHROOMS

Mushrooms are a potent source of goodness. The most commonly eaten varieties are packed with vitamin B for strength and fibre for keeping the organs flushing freely and blood-sugar levels calm. There are hundreds of types, and the edible ones balance the three major energy-giving nutrients: protein, fat and carbohydrates. Many vegetarians substitute mushrooms for meat as they are so full of iron. And adding mushrooms to meat is like having a triple shot of espresso, only much healthier. The 'high' will be genuine and last for a lot longer.

MUSHROOMS TO KNOW ABOUT

PORTOBELLO: These large mushrooms could make a nice shelter for a small frog, they are that big. They are round and flat, very white on top and very dark brown underneath. They are often used in veggie burgers as they are about the size of a meat pattie and are chewy, salty and hearty in taste and texture.

CREMINI: Also known as Baby Bella, these neat mushrooms are a more classic shape and size than portobello and shitake 'shrooms. They are the perfect little house shape of the standard white button mushroom, though should be a gentle shade of brown and a little darker around the edges. They have an earthy taste and go delightfully crisp and buttery when sauteed lightly in olive oil — it's not necessary to add cream, though that can be an indulgent topping especially when loaded with ground pepper. Their cute secret is: they are actually baby portobellos that have not been allowed to grow to full size.

SHITAKE: These are curiously shaped — more floppy and delicate than the others, and no two shitakes look quite alike. Their taste is a bit meaty and they can have a hint of shallot flavour to them. Shitakes add a perfect salty taste to many Asian dishes and also go beautifully in a creamy sauce topped over noodles. They also contain a substance called D-eritadenine, which is not in other mushrooms and helps lower cholesterol and support cardiovascular health.

RAW OR COOKED?

The nutritional value of mushrooms is well retained in the cooking process so there is little lost when throwing the mushrooms in the pan for 3 to 6 minutes to get them juicy and nicely browned — adding a handful of parsley for seasoning is about all that's needed for a quick bite. In fact, there's a slight advantage to cooking: mushrooms retain moisture, which is drained or steamed out in the cooking process so more mushrooms are needed to cover a piece of toast or a bowl of fettucine. Therefore, the nutrient value will be doubled in the cooking process. Tricky!

Roast Pork Fillet with Mushroom Sauce

ROASTED TO PERFECTION AND SERVED WITH A CLASSIC CREAMY
SAUCE, PORK FILLET IS THE HERO OF THIS RECIPE

SERVES 4

1kg (2lb) boneless pork
fillet

2 tbsps olive oil

Freshly ground salt and
pepper

2 tbsps butter

2 cloves garlic, minced

1 medium brown onion,
chopped

250g (9oz) Swiss
mushrooms, sliced

½ tsp cornflour

2 tbsps white wine

2 tbsps American
mustard

1 tbsp sage leaves,
finely chopped

1 cup (250ml, 8fl oz)
vegetable stock

1 cup (250ml, 8fl oz)
thickened cream

3 sprigs fresh sage, to
garnish

Preheat oven to 180°C (350°F, Gas Mark 4).

Brush the loin with 1 tablespoon of olive oil and then give it a few
generous grinds of salt and pepper.

Place the loin in a large roasting dish and drizzle over another
tablespoon of olive oil. Cover with a sheet of foil and roast in the
oven for 30 minutes. Remove the foil (saving for later) and cook for a
further 15 minutes. Remove the pork from the oven, cover again with
the foil and let stand for 10 minutes.

SAUCE

Heat butter in a medium saucepan over medium-high heat until it
starts to foam. Add the garlic, onions and mushrooms and cook for
8 minutes, stirring occasionally until the onions have softened and
the mushrooms have browned slightly. Add the cornflour and stir
quickly to mix it through. Cook for 1 minute further.

Mix in the white wine and stir through. Then stir through the
mustard and chopped sage. Gradually stir in the stock and bring
to a boil. Reduce the heat and simmer for 8 minutes or until it has
reduced by about half. Mix through the cream and reheat until
just simmering. Do not bring to a boil. Gently cook for another 5
minutes. Season with salt and pepper to taste.

Slice the roast and add any juices to the sauce. Serve the slices topped
with the mushroom sauce and garnished with sage sprigs.

Mini Autumn Tarts

MUSHROOMS CONTAIN VERY MUCH GOOD STUFF AND VERY LITTLE BAD STUFF, SO THERE'S NO NEED STOP AT JUST ONE OF THESE!

MAKES 12

2 tbsps unsalted butter

1 clove garlic, minced

2 spring onions, thinly sliced

350g (12oz) mixed Swiss and button mushrooms, sliced

1 tsp Dijon mustard

1 tsp fresh dill, finely chopped

1 tsp fresh parsley, finely chopped

Salt and pepper, to taste

2 sheets frozen puff pastry, thawed

1 large egg, lightly beaten

1 tbsp thickened cream

30g (1oz) Parmesan cheese, grated, plus extra to sprinkle

Sprigs of dill and parsley to garnish

Preheat oven to 200°C (400°F, Gas Mark 6).

Lightly grease a mini tart or muffin pan.

In a medium frying pan, heat the butter over medium heat. Add the garlic and spring onions and cook for 2 minutes. Add the mixed mushrooms stir for 5 minutes until they have softened. Stir through the mustard, dill, parsley and salt and pepper to taste and remove from heat. Set aside to cool.

Cut the sheets of pastry into rounds that will fit snugly into the tart or muffin holes to form shallow tart cases.

In a medium-sized bowl mix together the egg, cream and Parmesan. Add the mushroom mixture to this and stir to combine thoroughly. Divide the mixture evenly between the tart cases and sprinkle with grated Parmesan.

Bake the tarts for 15 minutes or until the Parmesan is melted and golden.

Let them cool for 5 minutes, then serve warm with garnishes of parsley and dill sprigs.

Lamb Cutlets with Green Risotto

A LITTLE ATTENTION TO DETAIL IS ALL THAT IS REQUIRED TO MAKE THIS BEAUTIFUL WELL BALANCED DINNER

SERVES 4

CUTLETS

2 stalks rosemary

2 cloves garlic, thinly sliced

8 large lamb cutlets

3 tbsps lemon juice

¼ cup (60ml, 2fl oz) extra virgin olive oil

Salt and freshly ground black pepper, to taste

GREEN RISOTTO

6 cups (1.5L, 50fl oz) hot vegetable stock

2 cups (80g, 3oz) broccoli florets

2 cups (60g, 2oz) spinach leaves, loosely packed

½ cup (20g, ¾ oz) fresh parsley leaves, roughly chopped

2 tbsps mint, chopped

2 tbsps olive oil

1 tbsp butter

1 small onion, finely chopped

2 cloves garlic, minced

1½ cups (235g, 7oz) Arborio or short grain rice

½ cup (125ml, 4fl oz) dry white wine

1 tsp lemon juice

1 tsp grated lemon zest

2 tbsps fresh marjoram leaves, finely chopped

Salt and freshly ground black pepper, to season

Mint to garnish

CUTLETS

Strip the stalks of the rosemary leaves, place half of the leaves and half the garlic slices on the bottom of a dish big enough to hold the cutlets. Lie cutlets on top, then cover with the remaining rosemary, garlic, lemon juice and olive oil and season with salt and pepper. Make sure all the cutlets are well coated. Let them marinate in the fridge for at least an hour.

Heat a grill pan or barbecue to high heat. Grill the cutlets for four minutes on each side. Remove from the grill, cover with foil and rest for a couple of minutes.

GREEN RISOTTO

Heat the vegetable stock in a large saucepan. Once it starts to boil, add the broccoli florets and spinach leaves. Cook for 2 minutes, then strain out the broccoli and spinach, keeping the stock. Rinse the broccoli and spinach under cold water.

Place all the spinach and half the broccoli in a blender with the parsley, mint and ½ cup of stock and blend until smooth. Transfer to a bowl with the remaining broccoli florets and set aside.

In a large pot, heat oil and butter over medium-high heat until the butter is melted. Fry the onion and garlic for 4 minutes, then add the rice and cook for 2 minutes, stirring until rice is translucent. Add wine and stir until rice has absorbed it. Add all the stock except 1 cup to the rice. Stir the rice, cover and reduce heat to low. Cook for 20 minutes, stirring every 5 minutes or so.

Remove the lid and stir in half the remaining stock. Once it has been completely absorbed, add the puree and broccoli florets to the risotto with the remaining stock, lemon juice and zest and marjoram. Gently stir for another 10 minutes until the risotto is thick and creamy. Season to taste with salt and pepper.

Serve with the lamb cutlets on top and sprigs of mint.

Wholesome Stuffed Mushrooms

THESE HEARTY STUFFED MUSHROOMS BRING TOGETHER THE NAUGHTINESS OF BACON AND THE GOODNESS OF ZUCCHINI AND KALE

SERVES 4

1 onion, finely chopped

1 zucchini, diced

2 cloves garlic, minced

8 large field mushrooms

2 tbsps olive oil

4 rashers bacon, finely chopped

Salt and freshly ground pepper

2 tsps thyme, finely chopped

2 tsps parsley, finely chopped

1 leaf kale, chopped

1 tomato, diced

⅓ cup (40g, 1½ oz) mozzarella cheese, grated

⅓ cup (40g, 1½ oz) breadcrumbs

Sprigs of thyme, to garnish

Preheat oven to 180°C (350°F, Gas Mark 4).

In a medium bowl, add the onion, zucchini and garlic. Set aside.

Wipe down the mushrooms with a just damp cloth. Remove the stems and place the mushrooms on a large baking tray lined with baking paper. Chop the stems and add them to the vegetables.

Heat the olive oil in a medium frying pan over medium heat. Fry the bacon for 5 minutes until crispy. Add the vegetables from the bowl and season with the salt and pepper. Add the herbs and cook for 5 minutes, stirring every now and then. Add the chopped kale and continue cooking for a further 5 minutes. Remove the vegetables back into the original bowl.

Mix through the vegetables the tomatoes, mozzarella and breadcrumbs, ensuring everything is thoroughly combined. Divide the mixture into 8 portions.

Gently stuff each mushroom with filling. It should be sitting in a mound above the top of each mushroom.

Bake in the oven uncovered for 15 minutes until the cheese has become golden.

Serve hot and garnish with thyme sprigs.

Cheesy Zucchini Chips

SERVES 4

½ cup (60g, 2oz) Parmesan, grated

2 tsps parsley, finely chopped.

2 tsps oregano, finely chopped

2 tsps basil, finely chopped

Salt and freshly ground black pepper

4 small zucchinis, ends trimmed and quartered lengthwise

2 tbsps olive oil

Preheat oven to 220°C (425°F, Gas Mark 7).

Line a large flat baking tray with baking paper and lightly brush with olive oil.

In a small bowl, mix together thoroughly the Parmesan, parsley, oregano, basil, and a couple of pinches of salt and pepper.

Place the zucchini strips onto the baking tray and drizzle the olive oil over them. Sprinkle the cheesy herb mix over each strip, pressing gently.

Place into oven and bake for 20 minutes, until browned.

Serve while hot.

Tzatziki

SERVES 2

½ continental cucumber

2 cloves garlic, minced

1 cup (225g, 8oz) Greek yoghurt

1 tsp fresh dill, finely chopped

1 tsp fresh mint, finely chopped, plus a few fresh mint leaves

½ tsp lemon juice

¼ tsp olive oil

¼ tsp white wine vinegar

Peel and seed the cucumber, then grate it and squeeze out as much liquid as you can. Pat dry with paper towels.

In a medium bowl, combine the cucumber with the rest of the ingredients.

Serve with sprigs of mint as garnish.

ZUCCHINI FLOWERS

There are several edible flowers in everyday gardens and yet only the flowers of the zucchini plant have made it to the supermarket aisle. These are fun to eat — they are popular served lightly dusted in flour and pan fried or stuffed with goat cheese and laid simply on a plate. Eaten raw, they are crisp and gentle and have none of the bitterness of the zucchini. This is really getting back to nature and a delightful way to consume essential vitamins and minerals including zinc, magnesium, potassium, copper and calcium.

BLUEBERRIES

You can't go wrong serving up blueberries to friends at your next party. The humble little blueberry is a powerhouse. In just half a cup, it gives us the same amount of antioxidants as 2¼ cups of broccoli. Antioxidants help protect our bodies from disease and illness by waging war with so-called free radicals, oxygen molecules that damage our body's cells and are associated with cancer, heart disease and aging. So does eating blueberries keep you wrinkle-free and ward off cancer and heart disease? Maybe. Maybe not. But when something's this delicious, it's nice work trying.

Whatever the health benefits, it's indisputable that blueberries punch above their weight on the nutrient count. They are among nature's most nutrient-dense berries. Every cup contains 4g of fibre, 24% of the recommended daily amount (RDA) of vitamin C, 36% of the RDA of vitamin K and 25% of the RDA of manganese. When you consider that they are around 85% water, that's a lot of good stuff going on in the remaining 15%.

STORAGE TIPS

Fresh blueberries, especially if you buy organic, can be expensive so it's important you don't let them go to waste. Blueberries can spoil quickly. Most foodies recommend not washing blueberries until just before you are going to use them, to avoid the fruit going all mushy. Others advise soaking them for a few minutes in a bath of water (3 parts) and vinegar (1 part) and then rinsing before putting in the fridge. The vinegar kills off bacteria and mould ensuring that your berries don't quickly spoil for no apparent reason — and apparently they don't taste of vinegar as a result of this process.

Another great tip for good berry storage is to keep your berries on paper towel in the fridge. You can rinse and dry the plastic packaging that the berries came in, particularly if it is well ventilated with holes, and return the berries to it on paper towel. Alternatively, store in a clean storage container with the lid loose to allow moisture to escape.

If you don't plan to eat your berries in the next 2-3 days, then freeze them. Blueberries freeze really well. It's recommend to freeze them in a single layer first, so that the berries stay separated, before transferring to a container or ziplock bag for longer-term freezing. If you don't have time, they freeze just fine in a bag in the first place though. When berries are defrosted then can tend to be soft, so use them in cakes, pancakes and muffins or eat them frozen for a cool, crunchy snack. They will quickly soften in milk, so frozen berries on breakfast cereal can be a great summertime treat.

Glazed Blueberry Tartlets

SUPERFOOD BLUEBERRIES COMBINE WITH DELICIOUS CUSTARD AND CRISPY PASTRY IN THIS PERFECT SWEET TREAT

MAKES 20

PASTRY

1 cup (125g, 4oz) self-raising flour

60g (2oz) of butter, cold and diced

1 egg yolk

½ tsp vanilla extract

1 tbsp iced water

FILLING

¾ cup (200ml, 7fl oz) cream

2 heaped tsps caster sugar

2 egg yolks

½ tsp vanilla extract

150g (5oz) blueberries

GLAZE

2 tbsps mixed berry jam

Place the flour and butter cubes in a mixing bowl, and rub the butter into the flour with your fingertips until the butter is distributed and the mixture resembles damp sand. Add the egg yolk, vanilla and water and mix with your hands or a wooden spoon to combine.

Tip the mixture onto a lightly floured surface, and press together into a disc. Wrap well with plastic wrap and refrigerate for at least 20 minutes, or overnight.

Preheat the oven to 200°C (390°F, Gas Mark 6).

Roll the pastry out thinly. Cut circles from the pastry using a floured 5cm (2in) round cutter.

Line a mini muffin tray with the pastry circles, gently pressing the pastry to fit. Cover pastry with foil or greaseproof paper, and fill with baking weights (use dried beans or rice if you don't have any).

Transfer to the oven to bake for 5 minutes. Remove the foil and baking weights. Place the tarts back in the oven and bake for another 5 minutes, or until lightly golden and cooked through. If the pastry has puffed up, gently press it down with the back of a spoon. Allow to cool slightly, then remove the cooked pastry cases to a wire rack to cool completely.

Heat the cream over a low heat until it just comes to the boil. Remove from the heat. Whisk together the sugar, egg yolks and vanilla extract. Add a large spoonful of the warm cream to the egg-and-sugar mixture, and whisk to combine. Pour this mixture back into the saucepan with the cream and whisk to combine. Place over a low heat, and stir constantly with a wooden spoon until thickened. Remove from the heat, and pour into a bowl. Cover closely with plastic wrap and place into the fridge for at least 1 hour, or overnight, to cool completely.

To assemble, spoon the filling into the baked pastry cases. Top with blueberries.

To glaze the berries, heat jam until it liquefies. You can do this on the stovetop or heat in the microwave for 20 seconds. Brush the blueberries with a small amount of liquefied jam to glaze.

Mini Pavlova with Berries and Blueberry Cream

CRISPY, GOOEY, CREAMY GOODNESS TOPPED WITH BERRIES — FOR EXTRA ENERGY

SERVES 12

PAVLOVA

6 large egg whites at room temperature

1¼ cups (275g, 10oz) sugar

2 tsps cornflour

½ tsp cream of tartar

¼ tsp salt

½ tsp vanilla extract

1 tsp apple cider vinegar

CREAM

3 tbsps raspberry jam

1 cup (250ml, 8fl oz) thickened cream

TOPPING

2 cups (200g, 7oz) fresh blueberries, washed and well dried

Couple of sprigs of mint.

Preheat oven to 180°C (350°F, Gas Mark 4).

Line a large flat baking tray with baking paper.

In a large mixing bowl, or using a mixer stand, beat the egg whites until peaks begin to form. Pour in the sugar and continue beating until your meringue forms stiff glossy peaks.

Add the cornflour, cream of tartar, salt, vanilla and vinegar. Whisk through to incorporate.

Spoon out 12 portions of the meringue onto the baking paper. Make a small well in the center of each round, this will help with holding the cream and berries later.

Place the tray in the oven and reduce the heat to 150°C (300°F, Gas Mark 2). Bake for 30 minutes. Turn oven off and let pavlovas cool inside the oven for 1 hour. Do not open the oven until the pavlovas have cooled.

Add the jam to the cream and stir until well combined.

Spoon out equal portions of the cream into each pavlova, top with blueberries, garnish with a leaf or two of mint and serve.

English Trifle with Raspberries

PERFECT FOR A DINNER PARTY OR AFTERNOON BARBECUE WITH FRIENDS — THEY'LL NEVER GUESS IT TOOK FIVE MINUTES TO MAKE

SERVES 6

300g (10oz) sponge cake, halved and cut into thick slices

2 punnets fresh raspberries (save about 8 for garnish)

2 cups (500ml, 1pt) thickened custard

2 cups (500ml, 1pt) thickened cream

1 tbsp caster sugar

1 tsp vanilla extract

4 sprigs mint leaves

Line 6 dessert bowls with slices of the sponge cake — divide it evenly between the bowls.

Spoon half the custard over the sponge in each bowl.

Divide the raspberries evenly among the bowls and place more custard on top.

In a separate large bowl, whip the cream with the sugar and vanilla extract until soft peaks form. You don't want it too thick, it needs to still be slightly creamy.

Spoon the cream over the custard and top with a dollop of custard.

Decorate each trifle with reserved raspberries and mint sprigs.

Let sit in the fridge for at least 4 hours before serving to let the custard soak into the sponge.

Green Tea Panna Cotta

YOUR GUESTS WILL LOVE YOU FOR BREAKING THE RULES WITH THIS JAPANESE - ITALIAN INFLUENCED PANNA COTTA

SERVES 4

2 cups (500ml, 1pt) milk

2 cups (500ml, 1pt) thickened cream

75g (3oz) caster sugar

2 tsp (7g, ¼ oz) powdered gelatin

1 tbsp matcha green tea plus extra to sprinkle

½ cup (50g, 2oz) fresh berries, to serve

In a large saucepan, heat the milk, cream and sugar over medium heat, gently whisking until the sugar has dissolved (you shouldn't be able to feel the granules at the bottom of the pan with your whisk).

Soften the gelatin powder in 1 tablespoon of cold water in a small bowl, then add to the hot milk and mix through. Remove from heat briefly while you complete the next step.

In a small bowl, stir 2 tablespoons of the hot milk mix into the matcha until it becomes a smooth paste, then add another 2 tablespoons to make it a thick liquid. Slowly pour the matcha mix back into the hot milk, whisking the whole time.

Place the saucepan back over medium heat, and whisk every now and then until it's about to simmer.

Reduce the heat to low and keep cooking for 5-10 minutes, or until the matcha and gelatin are completely dissolved.

Carefully transfer the liquid into four panna cotta moulds and refrigerate for at least 2 hours until set.

To remove the panna cotta, briefly dip each mould base in hot water for about 10 seconds. Carefully invert onto your serving plate and it should slide out with a couple of gentle shakes.

Serve with a couple of fresh berries on the side and sprinkle ¼ teaspoon of matcha powder over the top.

Index

almonds 83
apricot almond balls 70
banana nut loaf 88
chocolate nut sunday 168
nutty apricot granola bars 72
raw carrot cake bars 90
apple
nut spice smoothie 180
apricot
apricot almond balls 70
apricot yoghurt muffins 70
dried apricots 71
fruit salad with couscous 40
nutty apricot granola bars 72
asparagus
asparagus and prawn bisque 250
avocado
chocolate nut sunday 168
eggs baked in avocado boats 26
the green day smoothie 162
bacon
farmer's breakfast 50
sweet and sour sauteed sprouts 224
wholesome stuffed mushrooms 282
banana
banana nut loaf 88
banana oat muffins 84
yoghurt and banana pops 84
barley
barley bean salad 216
beans
barley bean salad 216
bean dip 117
black bean and sweet potato quesadilla 102
cannellini 113
four bean salad 114
green beans 217
green bean salad 216
home-made baked beans 52
mung bean salad 116
white bean salad 116
beef
orange beef stir fry 133
Thai beef salad 142
beetroot
busy bee smoothie 170
berries, *see also* blueberries, raspberries
grilled strawberries 171
kiwi and berry smoothie 200
super berry smoothie 202
blueberries 291
blueberry chia jam 36
glazed blueberry tartlets 292
mini pavlova with berries and blueberry
cream 294
bok choy 161

broccoli 161
lamb cutlets with green risotto 280
Brussels sprouts 223
sweet and sour sauteed sprouts 224
sweet Brussels sprout salad 228
buckwheat 65
buckwheat energy bar 66
buckwheat porridge with maple
yoghurt and plum puree 34
buckwheat salmon patties 68
buckwheat with mushrooms 47
cabbage
soba noodle bowl 128
capers 229
caramel
peanut caramel chocolate bars 78
carrot
green lentil meatballs with
carrot spaghetti 138
raw carrot cake bars 90
zucchini and carrot fritters 18
cashews
cashew nut milk 164
nut spice smoothie 180
raw carrot cake bars 90
cauliflower
cauliflower and spinach fritters 22
cheese, *see also* feta
cheesy zucchini chips 286
farmer's breakfast 50
tomato omelette 20
chia 31
blueberry chia jam 36
detoxify smoothie 170
mango chia cups 32
matcha chia smoothie bowl 194
overnight choc chia pudding 32
super berry smoothie 202
the green day smoothie 162
chicken
chargrilled chicken legs 220
chicken skewers and mango salsa 260
lemon herb-crusted chicken breast 218
prosciutto stuffed chicken breast with
cucumber salad 256
chickpeas
chickpea stuffed sweet potato 98
crispy chickpea fritters 104
falafel lunch box 140
roasted honey cinnamon
chickpeas 96
roasted spicy chickpeas 98
sweet potato burgers 100
chilli
chicken skewers and mango salsa 260
tom yum soup 242

chocolate 75
chocolate gingerbread cake 80
chocolate nut sunday 168
overnight choc chia pudding 32
peanut butter chocolate
smoothie 184
peanut butter coffee brownies 76
peanut caramel chocolate bars 78
pumpkin choc chip bars 92
chorizo
chorizo breakfast burrito 56
cinnamon
morning coffee smoothie 186
nut spice smoothie 180
roasted honey cinnamon
chickpeas 96
coconut 33
pumpkin choc chip bars 92
turmeric coconut smoothie 180
coffee
morning coffee smoothie 186
peanut butter coffee brownies 76
couscous
falafel lunch box 140
fruit salad with couscous 40
cucumber
crunchy fresh quinoa salad 122
prosciutto stuffed chicken breast with
cucumber salad 256
the green day smoothie 162
tzatziki 286
eggs
egg cups with ham and tomato 24
eggs baked in avocado boats 26
farmer's breakfast 50
frittata with cherry tomatoes 24
polenta quiche florentine 146
savoury porridge with mushrooms 44
summer picnic loaf 120
tomato omelette 20
feta
summer picnic loaf 120
fish, *see also* smoked salmon
buckwheat salmon patties 68
Hawaiian tuna poke 270
raw fish 269
salmon cakes 248
salmon mousse tarts 258
sardines on rye with herbs 47
sesame seared tuna tataki with oyster
mushrooms 272
ginger
chocolate gingerbread cake 80
tom yum soup 242
goji berries 175
goji go go smoothie 178

ham
    egg cups with ham & tomato 24
honey
    roasted honey cinnamon chickpeas 96
kiwi fruit 198
    fruit salad with couscous 40
    kiwi and berry smoothie 200
    kiwi gold smoothie 199
kombucha
    kombucha mojito 263
lamb
    lamb cutlets with green risotto 280
    lamb kebabs with yoghurt sauce 238
    Moroccan lamb tacos 136
lemon 17
    lemon herb-crusted chicken breast 218
lentils
    green lentil meatballs with carrot
        spaghetti 138
mango
    chicken skewers and mango salsa 260
    crispy tofu mango salad 210
    mango chia cups 32
    red quinoa mango salad 118
    summer noodle salad 130
    tropical sunrise smoothie 182
matcha 191
    green tea panna cotta 298
    matcha chia smoothie bowl 194
    matcha mint smoothie 192
mint
    matcha mint smoothie 192
mushrooms 275
    buckwheat with mushrooms 47
    mini autumn tarts 278
    mushrooms on polenta toast 152
    roast pork fillet with mushroom sauce 276
    savoury porridge with mushrooms 44
    scrambled tofu with mushrooms 54
    sesame seared tuna tataki with oyster
        mushrooms 272
    spiced mushroom risotto 212
    sweet and sour sauteed sprouts 224
    vegan polenta pizza 148
    wholesome stuffed mushrooms 282
nectarine
    fruit salad with couscous 40
noodles
    black noodles 132
    black noodle salad 133
    cold noodles 127
    soba noodle bowl 128
    summer noodle salad 130
    Vietnamese prawn noodle salad 246
oats
    banana oat muffins 84
    nutty apricot granola bars 72
    pumpkin choc chip bars 92
    raw carrot cake bars 90
    savoury porridge with mushrooms 44

orange
    marmalade 153
    orange beef stir fry 133
    polenta syrup cake 152
pasta
    baked ricotta shells with tomato sauce 236
    prawn & pesto pasta 248
pastry
    glazed blueberry tartlets 292
    mini autumn tarts 278
    salmon mousse tarts 258
peach
    peach cream smoothie 176
peanuts
    peanut butter chocolate smoothie 184
    peanut butter coffee brownies 76
    peanut caramel chocolate bars 78
pear
    detoxify smoothie 170
pineapple
    tropical sunrise smoothie 182
pine nuts 249
    prawn & pesto pasta 248
plum
    buckwheat porridge with maple yoghurt
        and plum puree 34
polenta 145
    mushrooms on polenta toast 152
    polenta quiche florentine 146
    polenta syrup cake 152
    vegan polenta pizza 148
pork 231
    classic pork tenderloin 232
    pork schnitzel 228
    pork stir-fry 234
    roast pork fillet with mushroom sauce 276
potato
    farmer's breakfast 50
prawns 245
    asparagus and prawn bisque 250
    prawn and pesto pasta 248
    tom yum soup 242
    Vietnamese prawn noodle salad 246
prosciutto
    prosciutto stuffed chicken breast with
        cucumber salad 256
pumpkin
    peach cream smoothie 176
    pumpkin choc chip bars 92
    wild rice salad 214
quinoa
    breakfast quinoa bowl 38
    crunchy fresh quinoa salad 122
    red quinoa mango salad 118
raspberries
    English trifle with raspberries 297
    busy bee smoothie 170
    fruit salad with couscous 40
    matcha chia smoothie bowl 194
    raspberry herb crush 166

rice
    brown rice 209
    brown and red rice bowl 214
    crispy tofu mango salad 210
    lamb cutlets with green risotto 280
    rice and ricotta pie 150
    sesame crusted sushi cube 262
    spiced mushroom risotto 212
ricotta
    baked ricotta shells with tomato sauce 236
    rice and ricotta pie 150
smoked salmon
    salmon rolls 264
    sesame crusted sushi cube 262
spinach 161
    cauliflower and spinach fritters 22
    detoxify smoothie 170
    green cleanse smoothie 199
    lamb cutlets with green risotto 280
    polenta quiche florentine 146
    summer picnic loaf 120
    the green day smoothie 162
    vegan polenta pizza 148
    wild rice salad 214
sweet potato
    black bean and sweet potato quesadilla 102
    chickpea stuffed sweet potato 98
    sweet potato burgers 100
    sweet potato chips 262
tofu
    crispy tofu mango salad 210
    scrambled tofu with mushrooms 54
tomato 25
    baked ricotta shells with tomato sauce 236
    egg cups with ham & tomato 24
    frittata with cherry tomatoes 24
    summer picnic loaf 120
    tomato omelette 20
    vegan polenta pizza 148
turmeric 181
    tropical sunrise smoothie 182
    turmeric coconut smoothie 180
walnuts
    banana nut loaf 88
yoghurt 85
    apricot yoghurt muffins 70
    buckwheat porridge with maple yoghurt
        and plum puree 34
    busy bee smoothie 170
    goji go go smoothie 178
    lamb kebabs with yoghurt sauce 238
    tropical sunrise smoothie 182
    tzatziki 286
    yoghurt and banana pops 84
zucchini
    cheesy zucchini chips 286
    zucchini and carrot fritters 18
    zucchini flowers 287

First Published in 2017 by Herron Book Distributors Pty Ltd
14 Manton St
Morningside
QLD 4170
www.herronbooks.com

Custom book production by Captain Honey Pty Ltd
PO Box 155
Byron Bay
NSW 2481
www.captainhoney.com.au

Cataloguing-in-Publication. A catalogue record for this book is available from the National Library of Australia

ISBN 978-0-947163-48-8

Printed and bound in China by Shenzhen Jinhao Color Printing Co., Ltd

5 4 3 2 1   17 18 19 20 21

NOTES FOR THE READER

All reasonable efforts have been made to ensure the accuracy of the content in this book. Information in this book is not intended as a substitute for medical advice. The author and publisher cannot and do not accept any legal duty of care or responsibility in relation to the content in this book, and disclaim any liabilities relating to its use.

PHOTO CREDITS